Sarah-Jane advises on all aspects of Private Client law, with a particular interest in complex or contentious trusts and estates.

She is recognised as a “Key Lawyer” by Legal 500 for both ‘Personal Tax, Trusts & Executries’ and ‘Contentious Trusts & Probate’.

Sarah-Jane is a full member of the Society of Trust & Estate Practitioners (STEP), having previously won a STEP Worldwide Excellence Award (Trusts Law & Practice) and gained her STEP Diploma (Scotland) and Advanced Certificate (Trust Disputes), both with distinction. She is also a current member of the STEP Scotland Branch Committee and is dedicated to furthering the profession through STEP and other avenues.

Having previously achieved a First-Class Honours Degree in Mathematics & Economics, before entering her career in law, Sarah-Jane uses those problem solving skills alongside her private client experience to reach practical resolutions to disputes. She has hands-on experience in negotiation and mediation, and in 2021 won the Core at 20 Mediation Challenge. She regularly speaks about dispute resolution for trustees and executors, in particular on the many issues surrounding legal rights.

A Practical Guide to Legal Rights in Scotland

A Practical Guide to Legal Rights in Scotland

Sarah-Jane Macdonald TEP

Law Brief Publishing

Published 2022 by Law Brief Publishing, an imprint of Law Brief Publishing Ltd
30 The Parks
Minehead
Somerset
TA24 8BT

www.lawbriefpublishing.com

Paperback: 978-1-914608-13-1

FOREWORD BY LORD HOPE OF CRAIGHEAD KT

It has long been a settled part of Scots law that surviving relatives of a deceased have legal claims against the deceased's estate which are preferred to the claims that arise on intestacy and are not capable of being excluded by any will that the deceased may have left. Stair, in his *Institutions of the Law of Scotland*, attributed our law about legal rights to ancient and immemorial custom, anterior to any statute. As he put it, the right of a surviving spouse has its origin in the communion of goods between man and wife during their marriage. The right of the children flows from the natural obligation of their parents to provide for them. So the parents' ability to dispose of their means is restrained, so as to leave a portion of their means to their children. It is because the law orders and determines that this should be so that this portion is called legitim.

In modern practice, the system is rather more complicated that Stair's brief description might suggest. The way we live and organise our lives has changed greatly since his time, as has the way we live together in families. In some respects the problems that these changes have created have been resolved by statute. The portion of the estate to which legal rights extends no longer includes heritable property. A surviving civil partner now enjoys the same rights as a surviving spouse, and the entitlement to claim legal rights has been extended to adopted children and to illegitimate children too. Stepchildren can enjoy the same rights if they have been adopted, and children born to a surrogate mother can participate in the estates of their intended parents if the relevant procedure that the statute affords has been followed through. But there remains a wide variety of other problems which must be worked out in the context of each case as it arises. Resolving who is entitled to claim may be relatively simple. Establishing what portions of the estate that entitlement extends to may not be, given the variety of property rights of all kinds that we may acquire during our lifetimes. And there are many other things that need to be sorted out too.

This excellent little book provides a guide through these various problems which every practitioner in this field will welcome. It is, as its title indicates, a practical guide. It does not detain the reader with theories or explanations. It uses simple language and a clear, concise and logical layout. It goes immediately to each of the issues which it seeks to address. Yet it does not overreach itself. It recognises that easy solutions are not always available, and it does not attempt to deal with points that are best left to those with expertise in other areas of practice. So those who are seeking guidance can approach this book with confidence that the guidance that is offered here will be of very real assistance, as they work through to a sound solution to each problem and seek to avoid any pitfalls that they may encounter along the way.

David Hope
December 2021

PREFACE

With contentious executries on the rise, legal rights issues are at the forefront of many of the disputes that practitioners see. Professional negligence claims and actions against executors are likewise becoming increasingly more prevalent, so ensuring clients have the proper advice is pivotal.

Despite this, much of the law is outdated and judicial authority is ambiguous, fact-specific or lacking. Unfortunately, as many legal rights issues continue to be settled outside of the court, the law has stagnated, and practice has been forced to fill the gaps.

It has therefore never been more important to have a practical guide to legal rights covering the key principles, common issues, hidden traps and tax implications to watch out for. This book is therefore designed to collate the relevant law for practitioners. Whilst it can't provide answers to all situations, as every case will depend on the facts, it will hopefully serve as a useful checklist and foundation on which practitioners can build on.

The law in this book is correct at the time of writing at 1st December 2021.

With thanks to Lord Hope for his kind words and foreword; John McArthur and Agnes Mallon for their support and encouragement; and Emma McFarlane for her assistance with the book.

Sarah-Jane Macdonald
December 2021

CONTENTS

CHAPTER ONE

REMINDER OF BASIC PRINCIPLES

What are legal rights?

Legal rights is a concept unique to Scots law. It is a form of "forced heirship" that applies in Scotland to prevent testators disinheriting certain parties from their estate and has been described as "a very important check on capricious or unjust testaments"[1]. There is therefore no testamentary freedom as such in Scotland. However, legal rights are only calculated in relation to a deceased's moveable estate, so testators are, to an extent, free to dispose of their heritable estate as they wish.

In some other jurisdictions, certain parties may (or may not) be able to make a claim that they ought to be entitled to a share of a deceased's estate, and such a share may be at the discretion of a court[2], whereas legal rights are a set entitlement in Scotland. To some extent, this gives testators certainty as to what legal rights will be and allows testators the opportunity to undertake succession planning with legal rights in mind. However, there are a number of grey areas when it comes to legal rights.

Legal rights are a common law entitlement. Many of the cases are over 100 years old[3] and there is very little modern authority to provide practitioners with guidance.

---

[1] *Hutton's Trustees* v *Hutton's Trustees* 1916 SC 860, per Lord Salvesen at 870.

[2] For example in England and Wales, claims may be brought under the Inheritance (Provision for Family and Dependants) Act 1975.

[3] Authors have commented previously on the fact legal rights have pre-dated most modern law, with the origin dating back to Roman law amongst others, see: H Hiram, *The Scots Law of Succession* Tottel Publishing and J C Gardner *The Origin*

The Succession (Scotland) Act 1964 (hereafter, the "1964 Act") governs the distribution of estates under intestacy and does provide some legislative guidance on legal rights, but there remain numerous points on which there is no definitive authority.

This book is designed to highlight some of the key practical areas and pitfalls that can crop up in practice that practitioners should be aware of.

When do legal rights apply?

Legal rights apply to all estates where the deceased was domiciled in Scotland at the time of their death.

This book does not cover issues of domicile, but practitioners should take care to consider scenarios where domicile is not clear cut.

Assuming the deceased was domiciled in Scotland, then:

- If the deceased died testate, legal rights should always be considered; but
- If the deceased died intestate, legal rights will only come into operation if prior rights have not exhausted the estate.[4]

Under s 10(2) of the 1964 Act:

> "*The amount of any claim to [legal rights] out of an estate shall be calculated by reference to so much of the net moveable estate as remains* ***after the satisfaction*** *of any claims thereon under the two last foregoing sections [i.e. prior rights].*"

---

and Nature of the Legal Rights of Spouses and Children in the Scottish Law of Succession (1928) W Green, Edinburgh.

[4] It should also be noted that if a cohabitant of the deceased makes a successful claim under s29 of the Family Law (Scotland) Act 2006, legitim is calculated after the deduction of such a claim.

This means that any calculation of legal rights (for either a spouse / civil partner or issue) described in this book only applies to the estate left after prior rights have been deducted and it will not take into account any sums due to be paid from the estate in respect of prior rights.

Who is entitled to receive legal rights?

On a very simplistic level, the parties entitled are:

- Spouses or civil partners of the deceased; and
- Descendants of the deceased.

Under the current law, cohabitants and stepchildren do not have any entitlement to claim legal rights on their partner or step-parent's estates.

The spouse or civil partner's entitlement is referred to under the Latin maxim, "jus relictae" or "jus relicti", meaning the surviving wife / husband's entitlement respectively.

The share due to any "issue"[5], meaning any descendant of the deceased, is referred to as "legitim".

Chapter 2 of this book will go into further detail of the parties entitled.

How are legal rights calculated?

Legal rights are calculated on the basis of the "net moveable estate". There are three key parts to this:

1) Ascertaining what the gross moveable estate is;
2) Valuing the gross moveable estate; then

[5] See chapter 2 for a definition of "issue".

3) Ascertaining the allowable deductions to reach the "net" value.

It should also be borne in mind that legal rights apply to the worldwide net moveable estate, not just the moveable estate situated in Scotland.

When considering whether an asset is moveable or heritable, practitioners should consider how the asset would be treated under Scots Law if it was situated in Scotland. There is some useful dicta in the case of *Monteith v Monteith's Trustees*[6] particularly around sums owed and secured on heritable property in England.

Chapters 5 to 12 of this book go into further detail on ascertaining the net moveable estate and the issues that can crop up in this regard.

Once the net moveable estate has been ascertained and agreed, the entitlement will then depend on who survived the deceased:

- If the deceased was survived by a spouse / civil partner only, their legal rights entitlement will be 1/2 of the net moveable estate;

- If the deceased was survived by any issue, but not by a spouse or civil partner, the legitim fund will be 1/2 of the net moveable estate;

- If the deceased was survived by both a spouse / civil partner and issue, then the jus relictae or jus relicti will be 1/3 and the legitim fund will be 1/3.

Once the legitim fund has been calculated, how that is divided up between the descendants of the deceased will depend on two key principles, namely representation and collation.

[6] *Monteith v Monteith's Trustees* (1882) 9 R 982.

Representation

Under s11(1) of the 1964 Act, if a child predeceases their parent, but has descendants of their own, such descendants step into the shoes of their parent.

This applies through all generations, so a great grandchild could potentially be entitled to legal rights.

It is therefore worth bearing in mind that just because an executor or family members state that the deceased does not have any children, it does not mean the spouse or civil partner will automatically be entitled to 1/2 of the net movable estate.

Practitioners will need to clarify whether representation applies. There is a risk for firms if they fully distribute an estate and it later transpires there is a party entitled to legal rights under representation. It is the duty of the solicitor to ensure executors are properly advised on this concept and failing to do so can cause issues for firms.

Representation is discussed further in Chapter 2.

Collation

The second principle that may alter how the legitim fund is to be divided is that of collation. This only applies where two or more parties opt to claim their legal rights, in which case lifetime gifts can be taken into account in determining how the legitim fund is to be divided.

Chapter 15 will explain collation in more detail.

How are legal rights treated?

There is authority that legal rights are treated as a "debt", albeit postponed in favour of other creditors.

In *Naismith v Boyes*[7] Lord Watson commented:

> *"The legal claims of the widow and children are not, strictly speaking, rights of succession ... They are in the nature of debts which attach to the free succession after the claims of onerous creditors have been satisfied."*[8]

Subsequent cases have upheld this position, describing legal rights as "*simply a claim of debt exigible from the deceased's estate*"[9].

Although treated as a debt, legal rights are not deductible for inheritance tax (IHT) purposes; they are merely treated as a debt for succession purposes.

Because legal rights are treated as a debt on the estate, it follows that the executors have a duty to pay that debt before fully distributing the remainder of the estate.

How are claimants treated?

Whilst practitioners often use the phrase "legal rights claimants", it should be borne in mind that legal rights are an entitlement under the law and are not "claims".

For intestate estates, the right to jus relictae, jus relicti or legitim will form part of the entitlement that a beneficiary under intestacy is entitled to.

In testate estates, however, where a party opts to receive their legal rights, the position is different.

---

7 *Naismith v Boyes* (1899) 1 F (HL) 79.

8 Ib Id at 81-82.

9 *Sanderson* v *Lockhart-Mure* 1946 SC 298 at 299.

As legal rights are a debt on the testate estate, which, as stated is not a right of succession, legal rights claimants are not "beneficiaries" of the testate estate, as such, but rather creditors.

This position was confirmed in *Moss' Trustees v Moss*[10]:

> *"A widow is entitled on her husband's death to one-third of the free moveable estate left by him; for that amount she is creditor on the estate. She is not a beneficiary..."*[11]

Because of the nature of legal rights in testate cases, executors do not owe the same duties to legal rights claimants as they would to a beneficiary under the terms of the Will. The duty owed is to notify any potential claimant of an entitlement to legal rights[12] and to arrange payment of the debt once the sum owed has been agreed.

How are legal rights to be paid?

Legal rights are met from the estate in the same manner as other debts, which was confirmed in *Tait's Trustees* v *Lees*[13]:-

> "*the claim of the widow for jus relictæ must be made up, so far as the residue is concerned, out of the residue; next, if the residue be insufficient, then out of the fund which otherwise would be available for the general legacies; and lastly, if both these are inadequate, then to the extent required out of the subjects of the special bequests. This is the ordinary rule of ranking...*"[14]

---

[10] *Moss' Trustees v Moss* 1916 1 SLT 321.

[11] Ib Id at 323.

[12] The duty to notify is discussed further in chapter 4.

[13] *Tait's Trustees* v *Lees* (1886) 13 R 1104.

[14] Ib id, per Lord Craighill at 1,111.

Cameron's Trustees v *Maclean*[15] confirmed that legal rights are to be met from this order of payment, and that a party cannot insist on being paid from the moveables, alone[16].

A legal rights claimant is therefore only entitled to receive a cash sum equivalent to the amount of their jus relicti or their share of the legal rights fund. A claimant has no entitlement to any specific asset within the deceased's moveable estate[17].

How are legal rights dealt with?

In testate cases, a person who is entitled to receive legal rights can:

- Accept their legal rights entitlement;
- Discharge their legal rights entitlement (in life or on death); or
- Leave their legal rights entitlement undischarged.

These options will be discussed further in Chapter 13.

If a legal rights claimant is also entitled to receive a legacy or share of the estate under the terms of a Will, then they will need to elect whether to take their legal rights or their inheritance from the Will. This is the principle of approbate and reprobate, which is discussed further in chapter 14.

In intestacy cases, the entitlement to legal rights is automatic, but may still be disclaimed or varied in the same manner as any other entitlement to an estate.

---

[15] *Cameron's Trustees* v *Maclean* 1917 S.C. 416.

[16] Ib id, Per Lord Dundas at 419, who commented "*I cannot accept the argument …that a widow is entitled to demand one-third of the moveables specifically*".

[17] Ib id, Per Lord MacKenzie at 419.

What if legal rights are not dealt with?

This is an issue that will only apply in testate cases.

If legal rights are neither accepted nor discharged, long negative prescription applies, which means that they will automatically prescribe after the expiry of twenty years[18].

Under the Prescription and Limitation (Scotland) Act 1973, the prescriptive period starts on the date "when any right to which this section applies has become exercisable or enforceable"[19].

Generally, prescription will therefore run from the date of death.

In *Campbell's Trustees v Campbell's Trustees* 1950 SLT 82, Lord President Cooper stated:

> *"It is sufficiently plain that the normal* terminus a quo *for the running of the negative prescription against a claim of legal rights is the date of death of the deceased."*[20]

That said, if a person is not capable of exercising or enforcing the claim as at the date of death, there can be scenarios where the "clock" for prescription does not start until later.

This can be seen in the case of *Mill's Trustees v Mill's Executors*[21]:

> *"Had the present been the normal case therefore prescription would have extinguished the second parties' claim. But the Lord President [in Cambell's Trustees] goes on in the immediately succeeding passage in his opinion as follows: 'I say nothing of the specialties which may arise where a claim for legal rights is made in a case of supervening intestacy*

---

[18] s8 Prescription and Limitation (Scotland) Act 1973.

[19] Ib id.

[20] *Campbell's Trustees v Campbell's Trustees* 1950 SLT 82, 84.

[21] *Mill's Trustees v Mill's Executors* 1965 SLT 375.

> *first emerging sometime after the date of death of the deceased in consequence of subsequent unforeseen events.' In my opinion, a case of supervening intestacy does raise special problems which take the case out of the ordinary rule for fixing the* terminus a quo *for prescription.*
>
> ...
>
> *In the light of this solid body of authority it seems to me to follow that in ascertaining the* terminus a quo *from which negative prescription is to run* ***the material date is not the date when the right in question vests or accrues, but the date when a claim was first enforceable by an action.***"[22]

The key part from the judgment is that the "material date" is when a claim is "first enforceable". This will be particularly important in relation to minor or incapax parties, which are discussed later, where a claim may not be enforceable at the testator's date of death.

[22] *Mill's Trustees v Mill's Executors* 1965 SLT 375, 378 (Lord President Clyde).

CHAPTER TWO

WHO IS ENTITLED TO LEGAL RIGHTS?

Spouses / civil partners

A spouse or civil partner of the deceased is entitled to claim legal rights.

A spouse is a person who was legally married to the deceased at the time of death. This means that they had a marriage recognised by Scots law. The right of the spouse to legal rights is a common law entitlement.

A civil partner is a person who was in a legal civil partnership with the deceased at the time of death. The entitlement of a civil partner was expressly given in the Civil Partnership Act 2004[23]. As of 30 June 2021,[24] it is now possible for a civil partnership to be entered into between mixed-gender or non-gender-specific parties.

Issues may arise in practice in relation to parties that have separated or entered into a divorce or dissolution.

Effect of divorce, dissolution and separation

A divorce, in the case of marriage, or dissolution of a civil partnership, has the effect that the spouse / civil partner no longer retains any "legal rights" in the estate of their former spouse / partner.

---

[23] s131 Civil Partnership Act 2004, which reflects the common entitlement given to spouses.

[24] Civil Partnership (Scotland) Act 2020.

However, a divorce or dissolution is only final once there is a court order to this effect.

Prior to a divorce or dissolution being granted by a court, the spouse / civil partner retains their full rights under the law of succession, meaning that they are still entitled to their legal rights.

As legal rights will apply even if a Will is in place, some separated spouses or civil partners may take steps to avoid this.

Where practitioners are dealing with the estate of a separated party, it would be prudent to check whether there is or are any:

- Separation agreements in place;
- Lifetime discharges of legal rights; or
- Pre or ante nuptial minutes of agreement.

Separation agreements often purport to discharge legal rights within them; these are, effectively, lifetime discharges (which are discussed in more detail under Chapter 13).

Even if a separation agreement is not complete, parties may have signed lifetime discharges of their legal rights.

Parties may also have pre or ante nuptial agreements that set out provisions as to what ought to happen upon separation, and some will also include provisions for death. If any such minutes of agreement exist, practitioners should take care to review the terms carefully to ascertain whether there is a sufficient discharge of legal rights.

To consider whether any such discharge would be binding, see the discussion under Chapter 13.

<u>Planning for separated parties</u>

Where a separation is contentious or complex, it is not unusual that it may take months (or years) to finalise a separation agreement. During that time, practitioners should consider what planning may need to be undertaken to take precautions against legal rights in the interim. This may be by advising the client on:

- Requesting lifetime discharges from their spouse / civil partner; or

- Taking steps to reduce moveable estate via gifts, converting assets to heritable property, etc.

It will very much depend on what is appropriate for the client.

If, during the course of a separation, one party receives a terminal diagnosis, care should be taken to consider whether divorce or legal rights on death is "better" for the client.

> Example
>
> Mr A, has children to a first (now deceased spouse) Mrs A. Mr A had remarried Ms B and they are now going through a contentious divorce. Ms B's entitlement on divorce may be significantly higher than an entitlement if Mr A were to die before a divorce is finalised. This is because Ms B's entitlement on divorce may include heritable property, entitlement to pensions, and other assets that would be excluded when calculating legal rights. If Mr A has estate worth c. £2.5m, Ms B may be entitled to c. £1m on divorce.
>
> Mr A could gift (if completed prior to death) assets to his children or convert his estate to heritable property. On death Ms B's entitlement to legal rights could be greatly diminished and may only receive, say £10,000.

Depending on the client's aims and diagnosis, this may be preferable. If any gifting or other planning is being undertaken the tax implications of any such actions should always be considered and weighed against the benefit (particularly capital gains tax on gifting pre-death). If tax can be avoided or mitigated, such options may still be preferable to a divorce settlement that would see Ms B receiving a large sum that could, otherwise, pass to Mr A's children.

Likewise, if a practitioner is acting for a legal rights claimant where such planning may have been undertaken, it may be appropriate to ask questions around the gifts to ensure they were effective (see Chapter 6 for further discussion on gifts).

Marriage by cohabitation and repute

In Scotland there is a concept known as marriage by cohabitation with habit and repute.

This was abolished by s3 of the Family Law (Scotland) Act 2006, so does not apply to any relationships entered into on or after 4 May 2006.

However, it does still apply to relationships entered into before this date and practitioners may come across cohabitants that this may apply to.

A cohabitant can apply to the court after the death of their partner to have their relationship recognised, formally, as a marriage by cohabitation with habit and repute.

If successful, then it would afford the cohabitant the same rights as a spouse,[25] which would give the cohabitant a claim to legal rights.

That said, it may be difficult to satisfy a court that a marriage existed as it requires evidence to be led to show that everyone knew the cohabitants as being a married couple and not just cohabitants. Therefore, such actions may be disputed in practice.

---

25 Whilst not the topic of this book, practitioners should note that HM Revenue & Customs have suggested that marriages by cohabitation with habit and repute should be referred to their technical team for IHT purposes and will be reviewed on a case by case basis.

For prescription purposes, a claim to legal rights would not be enforceable until such time as a cohabitant has obtained the court decree recognising the marriage by cohabitation with habit and repute. As such, arguably, the prescriptive period would not begin on the date of death.

Bigamy and polygamy

The difference between bigamy and polygamy is whether it is an offence in the country of domicile to be in a polygamous marriage.

In the UK, it is an offence to enter into a marriage / civil partnership whilst still legally married to / in a civil partnership with another person (i.e. before a divorce, dissolution or annulment). Any such marriage / civil partnership would be void under the relevant offences.

It may be possible, however, for a person to have a foreign domicile where it is legal to have multiple marriages, in which case it would be deemed polygamous.

For legal rights purposes, as the deceased person must have a Scottish domicile for legal rights to apply, then only the first marriage entered into would be deemed "valid" and only the first spouse would have an entitlement to legal rights.

This can cause problems where there are competing domiciles at play, for example, if a person has a Sharia domicile. Where this occurs in practice, specialist advice is recommended.

Children of the deceased

The general position is that the "issue" of the deceased are entitled to legal rights from the deceased's estate.

Issue includes the children of the deceased and their children (see representation below),[26] including any child of the deceased (or grandchild as the case may be) in utero (provided later born alive).[27] However, issues may arise due to the assumptions of parentage or where there may be disputes as to paternity.

Assumptions of parentage

This book does not intend to go into detail on family law issues and practitioners should take care to consult relevant specialists if queries of parentage arise.

Generally, a woman who gives birth to a child is deemed to be the child's mother for legal purposes[28] even in cases of artificial insemination[29]. A child born to that mother will therefore have a legal rights entitlement to her estate, subject to adoption, discussed below.

If the mother (as defined above) was married or in a civil partnership at any time between the conception and the birth, then that party is presumed to be the second legal parent[30].

If the mother was not married, then a man would only be deemed the child's legal parent if:

- they took steps to be named on the birth certificate[31], or

---

26 *John Young and Others (Turner's Trustees) v George Turner* (1897) 24 R 619.

27 *Elliot* v *Joicey* 1935 SC (HL) 57; *Cox's Trustees* v *Cox* 1950 SC 117.

28 see K McK Norrie, *The Law relating to Parent and Child in Scotland* (3rd ed 2013) paras 3.04 to 3.05

29 "The woman who is carrying or has carried a child as a result of the placing in her of an embryo or of sperm and eggs, and no other woman, is to be treated as the mother of the child" (Human Fertilisation and Embryology Act 2008, s 33).

30 s5 Law Reform (Parent and Child) (Scotland) Act 1986.

31 Ib id s5(1)(b).

- they obtain a court order declaring that they are the legal father[32].

Issues of paternity

Disputes can arise as to a child's paternity.

If the mother's name, alone, was on the birth certificate and there is no second parent noted, there is potential for a person to claim the deceased was their legal father. The onus would be on the claimant to prove this was the case.

Another situation that may arise is where a father has been listed on the birth certificate, or where he was married to the legal mother, but there is a dispute as to whether he is, in fact, the biological parent. In this scenario, the onus will be on the parties seeking to challenge the legitimacy of such a presumption.

The main way to assert or dispute such parentage would, ideally, be by way of having a DNA test carried out. Such a DNA test will generally give a clear result of either "positive" or "negative" to determine whether the deceased was the biological father.

Unfortunately, this is often not possible after a death, unless the deceased or other close family members had the foresight to have a DNA test undertaken to be used as comparison.

An alternative would be to test "siblingship". This requires a "known" child of the deceased to provide a DNA sample to be tested against the DNA of the "unknown" child. Ideally, the other parent of the children should be tested obtain as accurate a result as possible. These results consider the "probability of relatedness" and provide a percentage scale of that probability, which mean they are, arguably, inconclusive.

---

[32] Ib id s5(3).

If a DNA test is not possible, or if another party refuses to consent to the test, it is possible to raise a court action seeking a Declarator of Parentage. The court will then make a decision.

The court has power to request a party to the proceedings to:

1) provide a sample of blood or other body fluid or of body tissue for the purpose of laboratory analysis; or

2) consent to the taking of such a sample from a child in relation to whom the party has power to give such consent.[33]

Whilst the court can make this request, it cannot be enforced "for this would involve a person being subjected to a bodily interference, however slight, without his or her consent".[34]

If a party refuses or fails to provide (or consent to the taking of) a sample, adverse inferences may be drawn by the court as a result of those actions.[35]

In practice, the cost of obtaining DNA testing or seeking a decision by a court ought to be weighed against all the circumstances. Often such matters are settled out of court by way of an agreement amongst all parties.

Adopted children

Under section 23(1) of the 1964 Act, "an adopted person shall be treated as the child of the adopter and not as the child of any other person".

---

[33] s70(1) Law Reform (Miscellaneous Provisions) (Scotland) Act 1990,.

[34] A B Wilkinson and Kenneth McK Norrie, *The Law Relating to Parent & Child in Scotland* (3rd edn, W Green 2013) 3.31.

[35] Law Reform (Miscellaneous Provisions) (Scotland) Act 1990, s70(2); see also *Smith v Greenhill* 1994 SLT (Sh Ct) 22.

This applies to all deaths on or after the commencement of the act and as legal rights prescribe after twenty years, it will apply to all current legal rights claims.

This section means that an adopted child will have a legal rights entitlement in relation to their adopted parent's or parents' estate(s).

If only formally adopted by one parent, who later marries the second parent, that adopted child will be treated as a stepchild of the second parent and will have no legal rights entitlement to their estate.

It also follows from this section that an adopted child has no entitlement to legal rights from their birth mother's estate or the estate of anyone presumed to be the second parent at the time of the birth.

Stepchildren

At present, stepchildren have no entitlement to legal rights in a step-parent's estate, unless they were legally adopted by that step-parent. This applies even if the stepchild was raised as the child of the step-parent and accepted as a child under the meaning of an "accepted child" for family law purposes.

That said, the Scottish Law Commission's Consultation on Succession, which closed in 2019 did seek views on whether stepchildren ought to be given any such rights, so the position may change in the future.

Foster children

In Scotland, "foster care" refers to arrangements where a child under 16is looked after by someone who is not their birth parent; this may be under a "private fostering" arrangement or an approved foster carer.

Where children under 16 are looked after by a close relative, those relatives are referred to as "kinship carers".

Unlike adoption, foster care or kinship care is temporary (although it may be long-term if in the best interests of the child), so it will end when the child either reaches majority, returns to their birth parents, or is adopted.

As such, foster children or children in kinship care do not obtain any rights of succession to a foster or kinship carer's estate, even if they remained with that carer for the majority of their childhood (and into adulthood).

Children born via surrogacy

In Scotland, surrogacy is legal. However, there is a quirk whereby the "intended parents" of the child do not become a legal parent of the child until they have obtained a parental order to this effect[36].

This means that the surrogate mother is the legal mother of the child, regardless of whether she has any biological link to the child.[37]

Likewise, if the surrogate mother was married or in a civil partnership and their spouse / civil partner consented to the surrogacy, that spouse / civil partner will be the legal father or second female legal parent.[38]

This means that a child born to a surrogate mother who is married or in a civil partnership would have the same rights in succession as any other child if that surrogate mother or other parent pre-deceased an order severing that legal tie.

The child will not have any rights of succession to the "intended parents", even if they are the biological parents to that child, until and unless there is a court order to that effect or unless the biological father obtained rights through other means (i.e. where the surrogate is unmarried and they have taken steps to be legally recognised as the father).

---

[36] ss54 and 54A Human Fertilisation and Embryology Act 2008.

[37] Ib Id, s33.

[38] ibid, ss35 and 42.

This is a complex area of the law and specialist family law advice ought to be taken to ascertain succession rights if this arises in practice.

It should also be noted that the Law Commission of England and Wales and the Scottish Law Commission opened a joint consultation on these matters in 2019, which considers issues on legal rights[39]. The Surrogacy project has, however, been delayed and is not expected to complete until 2022.

Representation

As stated in Chapter 1, the principle of representation (under s 11(1) of the 1964 Act) applies to allow the children of a predeceasing parent to inherit the share of an estate that would otherwise have been due to the pre-deceasing party[40].

As also explained earlier, representation continues through the generations, so it also follows that grandchildren, great-grandchildren and further descendants could potentially be entitled to legal rights[41].

Representation only applies, however, where the person entitled to claim legal rights predeceased the deceased. If the person entitled to claim legal rights survived the deceased, but died before receiving their legal rights, representation does not apply. In such cases, it will fall to the executors of the deceased to claim or discharge legal rights.

Chapter 13 will discuss lifetime discharges of legal rights, which create the legal fiction that the person predeceased the deceased. For

---

39 Law Commission & Scottish Law Commission, "Building families through surrogacy: a new law", at 17.48.

40 Representation did not exist under the common law prior to the 1964 Act, this was included within the Act following recommendations in the Mackintosh Committee, *Law of Succession in Scotland: Report of the Committee of Inquiry* (Cmd 8144, 1951).

41 See *Turner's Trustees* v *Turner* (1897) 24 R 619.

representation purposes, this fiction is irrelevant and the lifetime discharge will have the effect that representation will not apply.

Division of legitim fund on representation

Where representation applies, the division of the legitim fund will depend on who survived the deceased and what generational branch they are on:

- if all parties are of the same generation (e.g. all grandchildren, or all great-grandchildren), then the division will be on a per capita basis[42]; but
- if the parties are of different generations (e.g. there may be one child, and two grandchildren), then division is on a per stirpes basis[43].

Per capita division

Where all parties are of the same generation, then the legitim fund is divided equally between all parties.

Example: The deceased had two children A and B, both of whom predeceased the deceased. A had 2 children and B had 3 children. The five grandchildren are all in the same generation and are each entitled to a 1/5 share of the legitim fund.

Per stirpes division

Where the parties are of different generations, then the legitim fund is divided equally across those of the same generation, including the

---

42 s11(2)(a) 1964 Act.

43 s11(2)(b) 1964 Act.

predeceasing party, and then the predeceasing party's children will receive their share.

Example: The deceased had two children A and B, but only A predeceased the deceased. A had 2 children. The legitim fund would be divided equally between A and B so they would be entitled to 1/2 each. A's children would then receive A's share equally. The legitim fund would therefore be divided as 1/2 to B and 1/4 to each of A's children.

To put this in context, if the legitim fund is £9,000 and the deceased had 3 children, they would each be entitled to £3,000. If one of those children pre-deceased but had 2 children of their own, those 2 grandchildren would share in the £3,000 due to their parent, i.e. they would receive £1,500 each.

Illegitimate children

There is, under modern law, no discrimination against illegitimate children and they are afforded the same rights as legitimate children in respect of legal rights and representation.

This was not always the case, and a couple of dates to be aware of are:

- for deaths prior to 25 November 1968, illegitimate children had no entitlement[44];
- for deaths after 25 November 1968, but prior to 8 December 1986[45], illegitimate children were entitled to legal rights, but there were quirks for representation.

---

[44] s10a Succession (Scotland) Act 1964 (substituted by s2 Law Reform (Miscellaneous Provisions) (Scotland) Act 1968).

[45] Illegitimacy as a status was abolished in Scots law as a result of s1(1) Law Reform (Parent and Child) (Scotland) Act 1986 (substituted by s21(1) Family Law (Scotland) Act 2006).

CHAPTER THREE

ISSUES WITH CERTAIN CLAIMANTS

Common issues with claimants

Having identified that a party is entitled to legal rights, there are then certain issues that can crop up in relation to that claimant, including situations where the claimant:

- is a child and is not deemed to have legal capacity to make such a decision;
- is an adult with incapacity who may or may not have a party capable of making a decision on their behalf;
- has died after becoming entitled to legal rights;
- was bankrupt or sequestrated (or the equivalent in their jurisdiction) at the time they became entitled to legal rights (or became so at any time between the date of death and date of payment); or
- is missing and cannot be traced.

Claimants who are minors

Where young children have a potential claim to legal rights, the first point to consider is whether they have legal capacity to make such a decision.

Although the deceased was domiciled in Scotland, the children may be domiciled elsewhere, and it may be necessary to obtain a legal opinion on the age of legal capacity in their particular jurisdiction. Likewise, such an opinion ought to consider the ability of a parent or guardian to make decisions on inheritance on behalf of such a minor in that jurisdiction.

This chapter will only discuss the position in Scotland.

Children aged 16 to 18

In Scotland, the age of legal capacity is 16[46]. Therefore, any child of a deceased aged 16 or over ought to be informed of their entitlement to legal rights and afforded the opportunity to consider such a claim.

However, under s 3(1) of the Age of Legal Capacity (Scotland) Act 1991, a child can seek to have the transaction set aside any time before reaching age 21 where:

- an adult, exercising reasonable prudence, would not have entered into the same transaction;[47] or

- the transaction has caused or is likely to cause substantial prejudice to that child.[48]

This therefore means that caution ought to be taken when dealing with legal rights claimants aged between 16 and 18.

If a child is due to turn 18, practitioners should consider whether to delay seeking their views on legal rights until they have reached the age of 18 to avoid this uncertainty.

Children under 16

Where a legal rights claimant is under 16, they do not have legal capacity to make a decision as to whether to claim or discharge their legal rights. Where children under 16 have elected to claim legal rights over a legacy,

---

[46] s1 Age of Legal Capacity (Scotland) Act 1991.

[47] Ib id, s3(2)(a).

[48] Ib id, s3(2)(b),

the Court has allowed them to revoke that decision on the basis they were minors and the election was void[49].

A "legal representative" of the child, under section 10(1)(b) of the Children (Scotland) Act 1995 (hereafter the 1995), "shall be entitled to do anything which the child, if of full age and capacity, could do in relation to [the child's] property".

Under section 15(5) of the 1995 Act, a legal representative is defined as a person "administering any property belonging to the child; and acting in, or giving consent to, any transaction where the child is incapable of so acting or consenting on his own behalf."

As such, it may be possible for a parent or guardian of a child to claim or discharge legal rights on behalf of a child.

In doing so, the legal representative is "required to act as a reasonable and prudent person would" if dealing with their own property,[50] bearing in mind their "responsibility to safeguard and promote the child's health, development and welfare".[51]

A parent could therefore claim legal rights on behalf of a child under 16 under this legislation.

Technically, a parent, or legal representative, could also discharge legal rights. However, there may be queries as to whether that is what a reasonable and prudent person would have done. Provided the transaction was appropriate the legal representative would not face liability.[52] If it was not, then the legal representative could face liability.

---

49 See *Walker* v *Orr's Trustees* 1958 SLT 220.

50 s10(1)(a) Children (Scotland) Act 1995.

51 Ib id, s10(2).

52 Ib id, s10(2).

Where the person discharging legal rights on behalf of a minor child will receive a higher share of the estate under the Will, they will have a conflict of interest and that may impact on such liability.

Where practitioners act for executors, the executors may accept a claim or discharge on behalf of the minor child from their legal representative. The executors ought to satisfy themselves that the person is the relevant legal representative under the terms of the Act. In the event that the child, once majority has been reached, wishes to question the transaction, it would be the legal representative that would be required to satisfy the child as to whether the test that it was reasonable and prudent was met.

If acting for the legal representative of a minor child and advising on legal rights, practitioners should take care to consider any potential conflict of interest and advise clients accordingly.

<u>Payment to minor beneficiaries</u>

If a claim for legal rights is made on behalf of a minor child, a direction from the Accountant of Court may be required.

The responsibility to ascertain whether it is necessary to seek a direction is placed on the executor,[53] who is due to transfer the sum to the minor beneficiary and it will depend on the sum that is due to the beneficiary:

- If the value due to the child is over £20,000, the executor(s) <u>must</u> seek a direction; but
- If the value is between £5,000 and £20,000, the executor(s) may seek a direction, but it is not a requirement; and
- For sums due under £5,000 the executor(s) need not seek a direction.

---

[53] s9(2) Children's (Scotland) Act 1995.

Once a direction has been sought, the Accountant of Court may opt to transfer that sum to the parent or guardian to manage on behalf of the child until they reach 16. However, the Accountant of Court could require that the funds are managed by an independent third party and either:

- retain the funds until the child reaches 16; or
- seek the appointment of a judicial factor by the court to take control of the funds and invest the sum for the child[54].

Prescription for minor beneficiaries

As set out in Chapter 1, the "material date" for when prescription starts is when the action first becomes enforceable and, arguably, for minor beneficiaries who do not have capacity to raise such an action, prescription would not start until they reach 16.

As such, in practice this would mean that if a party is in utero at the time of the testator's death, prescription could be up to 36 years after the date of death and practitioners should take care where this may be the case.

Adults with incapacity

If an adult is due to receive legal rights from an estate, they can accept or discharge their legal rights as they see fit. An adult may not have capacity to make that decision; there are three key things to consider:

- whether the adult is deemed to have capacity in relation to this specific decision;

---

[54] Ib id s9(5).

- if the adult does not have capacity, is there a person appointed to act on their behalf who has the authority to make such a decision and agree / receive any sum potentially due; and

- who should the executor notify of such a claim to fulfil their duty?

Very similar to dealing with minor beneficiaries, the adult's jurisdiction will also have a bearing on answering these questions. For adults domiciled outside of Scotland, it may be necessary to seek a legal opinion on the laws relating to the issues set out above in that jurisdiction to ascertain how legal rights should be dealt with.

This chapter will only consider the position in Scotland.

In Scotland, the law recognises that capacity is not black and white and, as such, whilst an adult may be deemed incapable of making some decisions, they may be capable of making others. This book will not cover the intricacies of determining capacity, and as such, will only cover situations where the adult has been deemed incapable.

Where an adult has been deemed not to have capacity, it then depends on whether there is anyone legally appointed who can make that decision and who the executors should notify.

This book will consider the parties who may have powers to act on behalf of adults with incapacity and whether such powers extend to dealing with legal rights. Thereafter, it will set out the position where there is no one capable of claiming or discharging legal rights.

<u>Department of Work & Pensions "appointees" or "deputies"</u>

It is possible for a person (or company) to apply to the Department of Work & Pensions ("DWP"), to be deemed an "appointee" or "deputy" for the purpose of dealing with benefits due from the DWP on behalf of an adult with incapacity.

Often, if this is the adult's only source of income, this may be preferable to seeking a guardianship if that is not required for any other purpose.

There are, however, no powers that would allow a DWP appointee or deputy to make decisions regarding legal rights on behalf of an adult with incapacity. Their powers are restricted to collecting benefits, spending such funds on behalf of the adult, and liaising with the DWP on eligibility for benefits.

Lay persons may not be aware that being a DWP appointee / deputy does not enable them to deal with the adult's finances beyond that remit. There can also be confusion as a "deputy" or someone with a "deputyship" in other jurisdictions is the equivalent to a guardian or guardianship in Scotland and lay persons may not appreciate the distinction.

Practitioners should therefore take care to (a) obtain evidence from anyone purporting to be able to make such decisions that they do have the authority to do so, and (b) avoid disclosing information to a DWP appointee / deputy during such discussions which they are not entitled to.

If the adult only has a DWP appointee or deputy acting for them, there will be no one capable of claiming or discharging legal rights. This is discussed further, below.

Notifying a DWP appointee or deputy does not fulfil the executors' duty to notify a party of legal rights since they have no authority to deal with such a claim. The duty to notify is discussed further later.

Power of Attorney

If an adult granted a Power of Attorney, which is valid under Scots law and registered with the Office of the Public Guardian, it may give a financial attorney power to make such a decision on behalf of the adult.

This, however, will depend on the specific wording of the Power of Attorney document and the powers given to the attorney.

The powers ought to cover the ability to claim or discharge the entitlement to legal rights, to agree the sum due to the adult, and to receive such funds on behalf of the adult. If the intention is to discharge legal rights and it has been over two years since the deceased's date of death, such a discharge is also a gift for inheritance tax purposes and would therefore also require the attorney to have power to make gifts.

As an attorney can only act within the powers granted, if the Power of Attorney does not provide sufficient power to deal with the legal rights entitlement in full, it may be necessary to obtain an Intervention Order for one or more additional powers.

Guardianships

As with Powers of Attorney, if a Guardianship has been granted, it may give the financial guardian powers to make decisions on legal rights on behalf of the adult.

Depending on the adult's position when the guardianship was applied for, it may not give a guardian full powers to deal with legal rights. The powers required will be the same as those mentioned for attorneys immediately above.

In the event a Guardianship does not provide sufficient powers, then guardians can seek a variation of the Guardianship Order via the court. Unfortunately, when seeking a variation, as there is often no "welfare" element, legal aid will not be available. If acting for a guardian, the cost of seeking a variation ought to be weighed against the benefit of the legal rights sum due.

Depending on the timing for renewal of the Guardianship, it may be preferable to wait for such renewal and to seek additional powers on the renewal under legal aid. This will depend upon the circumstances and specific advice should be sought.

Directions from a sheriff

There may be situations where the attorney or guardian for the adult is not best placed to make a decision on legal rights.

This may arise if they are also the residuary beneficiary of the estate and there is a (sometimes perceived) conflict of interest. Another scenario may be if an adult with incapacity is in care and discharging their legal rights could be a deprivation of capital[55].

In such scenarios it is competent to seek directions from a sheriff. It is often best to set out the proposed course of action, the reasons for the proposal taking into account the guiding principles, and to ask the sheriff to approve that course of action.

It may be competent, depending on the circumstances, for a joint application for directions to be made between the executors of the estate and the attorney / guardian, which would ensure that the interlocutor granted by the sheriff directs both parties on how they are required to settle the legal rights position. Where a party is wearing both "hats", as it were, this would protect them from liability in both capacities. This may not be appropriate in all situations and specific advice should be sought.

<u>Prescription</u>

Much like with minor beneficiaries, an adult with incapacity is not capable of raising an action in relation to legal rights, and, as such, when prescription starts will very much depend on whether there is someone capable of making such a claim or not.

If there is an existing guardian or attorney, then the usual position will often apply, i.e. prescription will begin from the date of death, as there is a person capable of making such a claim.

In cases where there is no one legally appointed or where there is a person appointed but they lack the relevant powers to deal with such a claim, the position is less clear.

---

[55] This book will not cover the concept of deprivation of capital in detail, but, essentially, if a party deliberately deprives themselves of capital to avoid such capital being used toward care costs, a Local Authority can treat such capital, in certain circumstances as notional capital held by the adult or can seek payment from other parties.

Relying on the authority cited in Chapter 1,[56] the prescriptive period cannot begin until a claim is enforceable. As an adult with incapacity cannot enforce such a claim, arguably, the prescriptive period could not start until a person is *legally* appointed to enforce the claim. In the event that there is no guardian appointed during the adult's lifetime, this could have the effect where prescription would not start until the adult's death, when executors step into the adult's shoes.

This could mean that legal rights would not prescribe until years after the testator's death.

If an attorney or guardian has been appointed who has some but not all of the powers required to deal with legal rights, but have powers to raise actions on behalf of the adult, it is unclear whether a court would deem this as meaning that a claim is enforceable and that, therefore, prescription would apply in the usual manner. This author is unaware of any such authority on this point and, as such, if practitioners are advising an attorney or guardian on whether the ability to claim legal rights has prescribed, it may be prudent to obtain an opinion from counsel on this point, particularly if there is a significant value due to the adult.

<u>No one capable of claiming or discharging</u>

In the event that an adult with incapacity does not have an attorney or guardian capable of dealing with their legal rights, and there is not a party willing to apply to the court for a Guardianship, the executors cannot discharge their duties to notify the legal rights claimant or to settle the "debt" due to the adult.

On the adult's death, their executors will become entitled to claim or discharge the legal rights entitlement, and the executors ought to notify the executors of that entitlement in due course. That said often executors require a practical solution in the meantime.

---

[56] *Mill's Trustees v Mill's Executors* 1965 SLT 375.

It may be possible to consign the funds with the Accountant of Court to retain until such time as a guardian or executor is appointed to make a claim.

Alternatively, it may be possible to obtain executors' insurance to cover a potential claim.

There may be limited circumstances where an insurer takes on such a policy given the almost inevitability of a claim by an executor in due course, but it does have some merit where claims are more remote (e.g. if close family members waive any rights to claim if they inherit from the adult with incapacity's estate, such that the chances of a claim are greatly reduced). As with any executors' insurance policy the cost of any one-off premium would be based on the risk.

Executors

Under the Latin maxim "eadem persona cum defuncto", executors of a deceased essentially step into their shoes, which means that the executor(s) of any party entitled to legal rights can either accept or discharge the legal rights on behalf of that person if such rights have not already been discharged in lifetime[57].

The fact that the deceased delayed in making an election whether to accept or discharge legal rights does not bar the executors from making a claim after the death[58]. However, prescription does not restart on the death of the potential claimant, so the executors will be bound by the same time limit as the deceased was. The exception to this would be if the claim only became enforceable on the appointment of the executors[59].

---

[57] See *Mill's Trustees* 1965 SC 384; *Campbell's Trustees* v *Campbell's Trustees* 1950 SC 48.

[58] See *Mackenzie* v *Mackenzie* (1873) 11 M 681.

[59] See earlier in this Chapter.

The entitlement to legal rights does have a value and ought to be included in the inventory of the deceased claimant's estate. As it is an asset of the estate, opting to discharge legal rights ought to be considered against those who will inherit from that estate. If discharging, seeking agreement from those beneficiaries in writing would be advisable.

Trustee in Sequestration / Accountant in Bankruptcy

There may be a scenario where the person entitled to claim legal rights is the subject of bankruptcy or sequestration or some other equivalent in their jurisdiction.

If the relevant bankruptcy or equivalent is outside of Scotland, practitioners should seek an opinion from the relevant jurisdiction on the implications of the bankruptcy on the entitlement to legal rights and the appropriate party or authority to notify and liaise with on agreeing the sum due and onward payment.

In Scotland, if a party is sequestrated or if they enter into a voluntary arrangement with their creditors, then it will be the Trustee in Sequestration, Accountant in Bankruptcy, or the supervisor of the arrangement appointed to deal with the individual's assets and creditors that ought to be notified (referred to as the relevant trustee hereafter).

The individual's whole estate vests in the relevant trustee as at the date of sequestration.[60] Their "estate" will include anything that they have an entitlement to. A party is entitled to legal rights as at the deceased's date of death, and, as such, if they are subject to a bankruptcy or similar at that date, their entitlement to legal rights will form part of their estate under this definition.

If a party becomes bankrupt (or similar) after the date of death, but before any sums are paid to them, the entitlement to the sums not yet paid will likewise form part of the estate under the above definition, so

---

[60] s306 Bankruptcy (Scotland) Act 2016, s 78(1) or Insolvency Act 1986.

practitioners should take care to not only ascertain if a party is potentially bankrupt at the deceased's date of death, but also prior to making any payment to them.

Where a party has no entitlement under a Will, but is entitled to legal rights, the relevant trustee can seek the payment of legal rights.

Where the party can elect to receive an entitlement under a Will or receive legal rights, the relevant trustee can also make a decision in that situation. If a party's entitlement is delayed or discretionary, but there is definite entitlement to legal rights in the present, the relevant trustee may be more likely to opt to claim legal rights. If a parent is aware that a child has financial difficulties, they may amend their Will to reflect this, but it cannot thwart the entitlement to legal rights, which the relevant trustee could still claim.

This can be seen in *Aikman (Smith's Trustee), Petitioner*[61]. In this case, Mr Andrew Smith was aware of his son, David Smith's, bankruptcy. He amended his Will to direct that no share of his estate be paid to his son if his bankruptcy remained undischarged, and directed trustees to hold the share, with various provisions to allow for payments to David's children and other parties. Andrew Smith predeceased his son. The bankruptcy was undischarged, and the relevant trustee claimed David's legal rights. The court held that although David could opt to take the entitlement under the Will, which was to be held for the future, the right to immediately claim legal rights vests in the relevant trustee, and allowed legal rights to be claimed, forfeiting the entitlement under the Will.

Lord Low commented:

> "*Now, when his father died the right of the bankrupt to his share of legitim became absolute—it became in fact a debt due to him by his father's estate. The father by his settlement could not deprive the bankrupt of the right; he could only offer to him a provision in satisfaction of it, which the bankrupt was under no obligation to take.*

---

[61] *Aikman (Smith's Trustee), Petitioner* (1893) 30 SLR 804.

> *I cannot think that the bankrupt—being bankrupt and his estates under sequestration—can reject a fund which is his absolutely, and which is immediately available to his creditors, and that to take instead a provision for his family or for himself, as the event may turn out, from which his creditors will be entirely excluded.*"[62]

As the entitlement to claim legal rights vests in the relevant trustee, the question for practitioners is then how to ascertain whether a legal rights claimant is bankrupt, or similar, to be able to notify the relevant trustee. The same issue arises with any party who is entitled to a share of the estate where there may be a relevant trustee appointed to deal with their assets and creditors.

The Law Society of Scotland does not have guidance on dealing with bankrupt parties. The Law Society of England and Wales has, however, prepared a guidance note on this topic[63]. This book will not go into such matters in detail, except to say that the guidance note suggested that whilst practitioners can ask the question, outright, it would be risky to rely on this information and that bankruptcy searches should be carried out.

As the relevant trustee may vest in the person's entitlement to legal rights after a testator's date of death, practitioners should also take care to ascertain their status at the time of payment or at the time of obtaining a discharge.

Legal rights claimants who cannot be traced

One of the most common issues potentially faced in relation to legal rights is claimants who cannot be located.

---

62 Ib id at 805.

63 "Bankrupt Beneficiaries", Law Society of England & Wales, 26 February 2018, https://www.lawsociety.org.uk/en/topics/private-client/bankrupt-beneficiaries.

This can be where there is a "black sheep" child and the family have lost contact with them, or if a predeceasing child had a child of their own and the family had no contact with that child.

As executors have a duty to notify those parties, and to settle the legal rights sum due to them, what is required in practice?

Ultimately, it will be much like dealing with a standard case for a missing beneficiary. The executors will need to exercise reasonable efforts to locate or trace the missing beneficiary, usually by instructing a tracing agent.

If a tracing agent is unable to find the person, and cannot prove that they predeceased without children, there are a few options available to executors, such as:

- obtaining an executors' insurance policy;
- retain the legal rights sum by the executors;
- distributing where the residuary beneficiary is also the executor;
- amending the executors to be the residuary beneficiaries and distributing.

Each is discussed in further detail, below.

In all scenarios, one danger to watch out for is the principle of collation and how that might impact on the division of the legitim fund if there is more than one party entitled to legal rights. This is discussed at the end of this chapter.

<u>Executors' insurance policy</u>

An executors' insurance policy can be obtained which will pay out if the person entitled to legal rights comes forward before the right prescribes. The one-off premium will be valued depending on the insurer's view as to the risk.

If you have instructed a tracing agent, it would be prudent to request that they provide a report on the investigations undertaken and why they were unable to find the person in question. This will be used by the insurer to consider the risk and cost involved with a premium.

Having such a policy will allow the executors to distribute the remainder of the estate after the payment of the premium with the comfort that if that person ever comes forward, they are insured / protected.

As the risk is that the person entitled will come forward before legal rights prescribe, insurers may want to ensure steps have been taken to adequately advertise the death. This would mean ensuring there was an obituary or death announcement in a newspaper, and perhaps notifications of death and seeking the beneficiary in their last known location.

Insurers will not always want to take on the risk and may not be willing to provide such a policy, or the cost of the premium may outweigh any benefit.

Retention of sum by executors

Where an insurance policy cannot be obtained, the executors have a difficult decision to make, particularly if there are parties keen to receive their shares of the estate.

Executors could distribute a share of the estate to the other parties, but ensure a sufficient sum is retained to pay the legal rights claimant if they come forward before their entitlement prescribes.

As the missing party is unable to review and agree or accept the calculation for legal rights, the executors would need to ensure that they do not overdistribute the estate to other parties.

Executors should therefore err on the side of caution and retain a slightly higher sum than anticipated to avoid any questions regarding overdistribution later.

Likewise, as costs relating to agreeing the legal rights sum are due from the estate and will impact on sums due to residuary beneficiaries, practitioners should consider who this will be dealt with in practice, either retaining additional sums to cover potential costs, or considering an indemnity to cover costs in this regard.

This sum can be placed on an interest-bearing account, or there may be an option to have it consigned to the Accountant of Court.

If the legal rights claimant comes forward prior to their right prescribing, their entitlement to legal rights can be dealt with in the usual manner. Any balance of funds not required for the legal rights claimant in that scenario, or because the right prescribes, can then be distributed to the residuary beneficiary or beneficiaries.

Distribution to executor and residuary beneficiary

If the residuary beneficiary is also the sole executor, they may wish to receive the whole balance of the estate. In that scenario, if a claim were ever made, the executor / residuary beneficiary (being the same person) would be personally liable to settle the amount due to the legal rights claimant,[64] but they may be happy to take on that risk.

If going down that route, it would be prudent to get the residuary beneficiary's consent in writing that they willingly accept the risk and are aware of the consequences to avoid any claims against the solicitors, as agents, in the future. An indemnity may be appropriate.

Amend executors and distribute

If the residuary beneficiary or beneficiaries are not executors, but want the executors to distribute the whole estate to them, similar to the route described above, the executors should be advised of liability.

As executors are duty-bound to settle all known estate debts, distributing the estate without settling all legal rights sums could mean that an

---

[64] This is because the executor would have distributed the estate without settling all known debts in breach of their duties, but as the residuary beneficiary and the executor is the same party, the incidence of liability is irrelevant.

executor would face personal liability if the legal rights claimant were ever to come forward and seek payment of the sum due to them.

Liability is joint and several between executors, and, as such, a legal rights claimant could seek to be paid by any one of them.

In that case, the executors may wish to resign and assume the residuary beneficiary or beneficiaries to act as executors in their place. As part of any resignation, it may also be prudent to include an indemnity in favour of the outgoing executors to avoid claims later, particularly as the outgoing executors are aware that the purpose of their resignation is to allow the incoming executors to breach their duties.

Danger of collation with missing legal rights claimants

A difficulty may arise if there are other legal rights claimants who wish to accept their legal rights in addition to the missing party. This is because the missing party would be entitled to request that the principle of collation is applied. Collation is discussed in further detail in Chapter 15.

The executors would have to assume that the missing party, if they came forward, would seek collation to apply, unless the executors can satisfy themselves that the missing party would receive less in that scenario.

The executors therefore ought to ascertain any gifts made by the other claimants before working out what sum each would be due if the missing party were to seek collation.

The other claimants would only receive the sum from the estate they would be due under the assumption that collation will be applied, then, after the twenty year prescription period has elapsed, the balance could be paid to them once it is clear collation will not apply. Careful records should therefore be kept as to what sums will be due to each party.

Alternatively, if the executors wish to pay out legal rights on the assumption that a missing beneficiary will not come forward and collation will not apply, when the executors pay the legal rights sums out, they may wish to include an indemnity that if the missing party does come forward and seek collation, the legal rights claimants indemnify the executors in respect of any additional sums that fall due as a result.

CHAPTER FOUR

DUTY TO NOTIFY

Having established that someone is entitled to legal rights from an estate, a question often asked is whether there is a duty on the executors or the solicitors acting to notify those persons of their entitlement.

General principles

The overriding principle to notify a legal rights claimant stems from the position that legal rights is, generally, viewed as a "debt" of the estate.

As noted in Chapter 1, legal rights are a debt and not a right of succession.[65] As executors have a duty to discharge all debts of the estate before distributing to beneficiaries, there appears to be an implied duty on executors to notify legal rights claimants of the existence of their entitlement.

That said, in *The Law Society of Scotland v David Haddow Campbell* (11 March 2013)[66] the tribunal concluded that there was no clear judicial authority that an executor has any specific duty to inform a legal rights claimant.

The case involved a solicitor, in their personal capacity, acting as sole executor of the estate and as agent. The solicitor was aware that the deceased had a son from a previous marriage who would be entitled to legal rights. The widow, who was entitled to the whole residue of the estate under the Will, did not want the son to be informed. The solicitor ingathered the deceased's estate then resigned as executor in favour of the

---

[65] *Naismith v Boyes* (1899) 1 F (HL) 79, 81.

[66] Full Finding available at https://www.ssdt.org.uk/media/44893/1576_campbell.pdf

widow taking his place as executor, whilst advising her of the son's entitlement. Due to the lack of authority at the time, the solicitor was exonerated. Professor Meston gave some interesting commentary which can be read in the full findings of the tribunal[67].

The Law Society of Scotland subsequently issued guidance stating that due to the nature of legal rights being a debt, it is their view that executors do have a duty to inform legal rights claimants.[68] The guidance goes on to set out how solicitors ought to deal with scenarios where they are appointed as agent or as executor and this issue crops up.

Lay executors

As it stands, there remains no cases heard on this point since the Law Society of Scotland's Guidance was issued. It is therefore conceivable that families who do not seek legal assistance in dealing with an estate may fall foul of this rule.

As there remains no judicial authority as to whether there is a binding duty on executors to notify claimants, there may be issues in a second-death scenario, particularly if the right to claim has prescribed, and potential claimants were not informed.

Arguably, there could be a case for breach of duty, and a court may take the same view as the Law Society of Scotland. Any action relating to a breach of duty has its own issues of prescription for raising a claim based on when the "loss" occurred and specific advice should be sought if practitioners are acting for a potential claimant in this scenario.

---

67 Ib id.

68 "Guidance Solicitors Acting as Executors and Agents" (*Law Society of Scotland*) https://www.lawscot.org.uk/members/rules-and-guidance/rules-and-guidance/section-f/division-i/guidance/guidance-on-solicitors-acting-as-executors-and-agents/> accessed 22 August 2021.

If advising the executors in a second-death scenario described above, practitioners ought to consider if there is any potential liability from the estate if a court deemed there had been a breach of duty and that sums may be due to the legal rights claimant.

As is often the case in dealing with legal rights, it may be that an agreement can be reached with a claimant to avoid a court action or an executors' insurance policy may be appropriate to provider cover and protection to the executors of the second estate (i.e. to protect against a potential action against the deceased for breaching their duty).

Professional / solicitor executors

<u>Where the solicitor / professional executor is sole executor</u>

The Law Society of Scotland's guidance confirms there is a duty on executors to notify all legal rights claimants of their entitlement.

Whilst solicitors or professional executors ought to provide residuary beneficiaries with a copy of any terms of engagement this does not confer any powers on the residuary beneficiaries to instruct the solicitor or professional executor. The guidance also reiterates that it is not open to residuary beneficiaries to request that executors do not advise legal rights claimants of their entitlements.

In *Cochrane's Executors v Inland Revenue*[69] it was noted:

> *"... the only directions which the residuary legatee is entitled to give to trustees or executors are in relation to the estate remaining in their hands when they have fulfilled all the prior purposes of the settlement and have otherwise completed the administration of the estate."*[70]

---

[69] *Cochrane's Executors v Inland Revenue* 1974 SC 158

[70] Ib id at 165 per Lord President Emslie.

As residuary beneficiaries therefore cannot instruct the solicitor or professional executor to do otherwise, it is therefore an absolute requirement that professional executors advise legal rights claimants of their entitlement.

Where the solicitor / professional executors are in the majority

There may be scenarios in practice where there is a lay executor appointed, but there are multiple professional executors. For example, there may be two solicitors appointed as executors with a lay executor, or a professional trustee company, a solicitor and a lay executor.

In Scotland, executors and trustees can make decisions by majority or "quorum" (if quorum is defined in the trust deed, it will prevail).

The professional executors may therefore have the majority or quorum required to make a decision, regardless of the lay executor's position.

In the same way that a sole professional executor is bound by a duty to notify, the majority of professional executors would be obliged to do so as well.

This can lead to complications where the lay executor does not wish to advise any legal rights claimants and it can sour the solicitor / client relationship if not handled sensitively.

Ideally, the professional executors would persuade the remaining executor that this is a legal requirement that must be undertaken. If the lay executor cannot be persuaded, the decision would require to be made by the majority and the legal rights claimants would have to be notified notwithstanding that one executor has dissented in that decision.

Where the solicitor / professional executor is in the minority

In cases where the solicitor or professional trustee company is only one executor, it is possible that a majority of lay executors may decide not to notify legal rights claimants of their entitlement.

The Law Society of Scotland has therefore recommended that such solicitor / professional trustees not only resign from acting, but also record their dissent to such a decision, which ought to be in writing and intimated to the other executors. The guidance further recommends that such written dissent also include a declaration that the quorum or majority have made a decision that does not reflect the legal position, which is the reason for the dissenting vote.

The general position under trust law is that if there is a breach of duty by the trustees, then all acting trustees are jointly and severally liable, and if there is a loss caused by that breach, they may be personally liable to make good that loss.

Although there remains a question as to whether a court would hold that such notification is a "duty", and that a breach of duty has occurred, practitioners may want additional assurance from their co-executors that they will not be held liable for any such breaches.

An indemnity by the co-executors in favour of the resigning solicitor / professional trustee could be signed indemnifying them of any loss if any such claim is raised at a later date. The terms of such an indemnity ought to cover the costs of defending any such claim in addition to any sums held to be due under the principle of joint and several liability.

The Law Society of Scotland's guidance then recognises that it is unclear as to whether there is then any moral duty on the resigning professional-trustee to notify a legal rights claimant. It is suggested in the guidance that there may be some endorsement for doing so,[71] but that there is no definitive authority on this point. In the meantime, on the basis that decisions can be made by majority, the resigning party appears to have no such obligation.

Where there is a "tie"

The worst scenario is perhaps where there is a "tie", in other words where the professional executors and lay executors are evenly numbered, and a

---

[71] *Frank Houlgate Investment Company Limited v Biggart Baillie LLP* [2014] CSIH 79.

majority cannot be achieved. This may be where there is a professional trustee company and a surviving spouse or a cohabitant, for example.

In such scenarios, there is no majority to reach a decision.

Unlike the scenario where a professional trustee is already in the minority and their resignation would not alter the action of the continuing trustees, if the professional trustee company resigns, where there is a tie, the result of such resignation would give the remaining trustee a majority. Such action would therefore allow the lay executor(s) to breach their duty. This can put the professional trustee in an awkward position.

One option, to avoid any suggestion of liability on the part of the professional trustee, would be to seek the removal of the lay trustee. The removal of an executor can be undertaken where necessary and if there has been some "malversation" of office.[72]

As it would be an expensive route to take, even if there is an award for expenses, it would be hoped that the suggestion or threat of such action would persuade the lay executor to "break the tie". If not, a professional executor ought to take advice on their potential liability of resigning and weigh this against a potential action for removal.

Solicitors acting as agents

Where a practice unit has been instructed to deal with the administration of an estate only and they are acting as agents, but no practitioner from the unit nor any professional trustee company associated with the unit has ever been appointed as executor, the above guidance will not apply.

The practitioner, as agent to the executors, will have a duty to advise on legal rights and the executors' duty to notify the legal rights claimants of their potential entitlement and ensure those executors are properly advised as to any breach of the duty and potential liability.

---

[72] *MacGilchrist's Trustees v MacGilchrist* 1930 SC 635.

If, after being properly advised, the executors instruct the practitioner not to disclose the entitlement to legal rights to claimants, and the executors are resolute on this matter, then the Law Society of Scotland's guidance recommends that practitioners obtain these instructions in writing.

The guidance goes on to suggest that practitioners ought to resign from acting in these scenarios.

The guidance recognises that if solicitors cannot act where such instructions are given it would mean that the executors could not instruct any firm. That said, the guidance compares acting in these scenarios as being tantamount to defrauding a creditor.

Practitioners' confidentiality will remain in place after a resignation and, as such, ought not to disclose anything after a resignation.

CHAPTER FIVE

ESTABLISHING THE MOVEABLE ESTATE

What is the deceased's estate?

Whilst legal rights only apply to the moveable estate, it is first necessary to establish what the deceased's estate consists of, to then carve out the moveable estate.

The 1964 Act defines the deceased's estate as:

> "...estate, whether heritable or moveable, or partly heritable and partly moveable, belonging to the deceased at the time of his death or over which he has a power of appointment."[73]

Generally, this means it will include any property that was *in bonis* at the deceased's date of death.

From this general definition, any assets or rights that the deceased held that are deemed to be moveable will form part of the moveable estate for legal rights purposes[74].

What is moveable property?

The simplest answer is that moveable property is an asset, right, or interest that the deceased held that is not classed as heritable in nature.

Broadly moveable property can be categorised as:

---

[73] s36(2) Succession (Scotland) Act 1964.

[74] *Beveridge* v *Beveridge's Executrix* 1938 SC 160.

- corporeal moveables
- financial assets
- digital estate
- rights held by the deceased / incorporeal moveables
- interests in a business
- certain interests in trusts – see chapter 6
- certain gifts made in lifetime – see chapter 6

The following chapters will deal with the latter categories above.

Corporeal moveables

A "corporeal moveable" is any physical or tangible asset that is "moveable" in nature, i.e. it is not fixed to the ground.

For legal rights purposes this will include:

- house contents and personal effects (antiques, jewellery, etc)
- works of art (paintings, sculptures, etc)
- collectible items (wine/whiskey collections, comic book collections, etc)
- vehicles registered in the deceased's name (cars, motorcycles, campervans, caravans)
- boats or aircraft registered in the deceased's name

The above list is not designed to be exhaustive, but is merely a guide as to what ought to be included.

If the asset was owned by the deceased, then it ought to form part of the moveable estate for legal rights purposes.

If household goods were held in a share home (i.e. with a spouse, civil partner or cohabitant), there is a presumption that such goods are held equally unless it can be shown otherwise[75].

For items on display in a museum or on loan somewhere, if the underlying asset belongs to the deceased and there was no intention for the item to be gifted, then regardless of the fact it is not in the deceased's possession at the time of their death it ought to be valued and included in the inventory and the legal rights calculation. There is, generally, a presumption against gifting in Scotland (chapter 6 will discuss this presumption and gifts in further detail).

Financial assets

Any cash-based assets or investments that the deceased held in their name are also moveable and ought to be included in the moveable estate for legal rights purposes, subject to a couple of exceptions.

Financial assets will broadly include:

- cash in GBP, any foreign currency, or travellers' cheques
- funds held in a bank account in the deceased's name (whether sole or joint)
- investments held by the deceased (stocks, shares, unit trusts, bonds, etc)
- national savings products

---

[75] See s25(3) Family Law (Scotland) Act 1985 and s26(4) Family Law (Scotland) Act 2006.

Chapter 11 will discuss valuation and the value to place on funds held where a bank account was held in joint names.

The financial assets that may be excluded from legal rights are:

- life policy proceeds
- pension lump sums

Whether they are excluded or not will depend on the facts and circumstances.

Life policy proceeds

A life policy is an insurance policy that will pay out on the death of the life assured. They can be set up in a number of ways, but the policy holder is the person who is entitled to receive the proceeds when the policy pays out.

If the deceased was the policy holder, the proceeds due will form part of the moveable estate unless the deceased assigned the right to those proceeds prior to their death.

To achieve this, the deceased would have needed to complete a formal assignation assigning the right to the proceeds to either: (1) a named individual, (2) a bare trust for another individual or individuals, or (3) to a discretionary trust.

In order for such an assignation to be "complete", it must be intimated to the assignee and also to the life policy provider. This is usually achieved by asking those parties to sign a document acknowledging intimation or to confirm it in writing.

If the proceeds are not properly assigned and intimated, they will continue to be payable to the deceased's estate and therefore form part of the legal rights calculation.

Practitioners should therefore be mindful of this point when advising parties on their succession planning and should highlight the possibility of such sums forming part of their estate (this advice applies equally for tax purposes).

Pension lump sums

A similar position applies to pension lump sums. Often these will be distributed at the discretion of the pension trustees, who will have two years from the date of death to make a decision as to the proper distribution of the lump sum. In making such a decision, the trustees will consider any wishes the deceased may have left (often in a nomination form or letters of wishes). Such entitlements therefore do not form part of the deceased's estate.

There can be scenarios where a pension lump sum has been assigned to a trust and a benefit is reserved to the deceased, in which case this can bring the pension into the equation. If that arises in practice, it will depend on the wording of the documentation and care should be taken.

Digital estate

A person's digital estate will include a wide array of digital information, access to websites or social media, digital photographs, online content, and so on, most of which won't have financial/monetary value.

Downloaded digital media

There is often a misconception that when a person downloads a video, book, or audio file, that they "own" that item and when a person dies they may have a large library of such files. However, what they own is a license to view, read or listen to that file, which cannot be transmitted on death. As such, even if there was a cash value paid for such assets during their lifetime, they won't form part of the moveable estate on death and won't impact upon legal rights.

The exception to this rule would be if the deceased owned the underlying rights to the video, book or audio file.

Cryptocurrency

Cryptocurrency is another area of law that is a minefield and this book does not intend to go into detail on it, except to state that cryptocurrency would be a moveable asset and ought to form part of a legal rights calculation.

Executors will require information on how to access the cryptocurrency, either with details of the key to a cryptowallet or details of the third-party provider who manages it on behalf of the deceased.

One area to take extreme caution with is the transfer or disposal of any laptop, computer or external hard drives that may hold cryptocurrency on them. If the executors lose or dispose the necessary access, it may result in the executors being unable to retrieve the cryptocurrency.

The Guardian has reported on a computer engineer, James Howells, who accidentally disposed of £200m in bitcoin that was on an old hard drive, and is now in a landfill[76].

Given the potential value of cryptocurrency this can be very dangerous, particularly as such value would inflate the legal rights entitlement for claimants and executors can be personally liable if they have not taken precautions to secure the cryptocurrency.

How cryptocurrency is valued is another matter and Chapter 11 will discuss this in further detail.

Cash-back or points

It is also quite common in modern times for people to have accounts with websites offering "points" or "cashback", whereby sums can be built up and traded for cash, vouchers, or assets.

---

[76] See: https://www.theguardian.com/uk-news/2021/jan/14/man-newport-council-50m-helps-find-bitcoins-landfill-james-howells.

If the entitlement to claim those points or cash transmits to the executors, then they will have an asset as it can be traded for money or money's worth and a value ought to be placed on it for legal rights purposes.

If the ability to claim points or cash ends on death and no right to claim transmits to the executors, there will be no value for legal rights purposes.

Incorporeal moveables or rights held by the deceased

Incorporeal moveables are essentially assets a person owns that have no tangible presence, but the deceased has a right to the underlying value. The financial and digital assets noted above are technically also incorporeal moveables (except physical cash).

However, it is worth remembering that any right that a deceased had that has a value or entitled the deceased to payments, will also be an incorporeal asset.

Such rights may include:

- intellectual property, unpublished works, rights for royalties, etc
- right to recover funds or actions for accounting
- right under agreements for payments, for example the right to repayment under a loan agreement
- right to damages for an action started pre-death[77]

There are some rights (not listed above) that may appear heritable in nature, but are actually deemed to be moveable and these will be discussed in Chapter 7.

---

[77] For example, rights to damages from breach of contract, see: *Morrison* v *Morison's Executrix* 1912 1 SLT 1834.

Funds held by attorneys

There are often situations where an attorney managed funds on behalf of a deceased and is holding funds on behalf of the deceased or had a joint account with the deceased that is now in their sole name.

Any such funds held by an attorney are due back to the estate and form part of the moveable estate.

In recent years, contentious executries have been on the rise and one of areas this can be seen is in relation to actions seeking attorneys to produce an account of their intromissions[78]. This is usually where one party had perhaps been sole attorney and managing the affairs of a parent for some time before death, and others entitled to the estate are seeking an accounting for their actions whilst attorney.

Attorneys owe a duty to produce such an account and if it transpires that any funds were not used for the deceased's benefit or cannot be accounted for, then such sums are due back to the deceased's estate.

This too will have a value that ought to be included in the inventory of an estate or, if not discovered prior to confirmation, ought to be included when calculating legal rights.

If you are acting for a legal rights claimant, and there are queries over the actions of an attorney, then suggesting an action for Count, Reckoning and Payment may be appropriate. Often, in practice, to avoid the cost of a court action, an attorney will produce a full account, but that is not always forthcoming.

[78] Actions for "Count, Reckoning and Payment".

CHAPTER SIX

INCLUSION OF ASSETS HELD BY ANOTHER PARTY

Are gifts or interests in trusts ever included?

There is often a misconception that if assets have been gifted to a third party or held in trust, they are no longer owned by the deceased and are therefore excluded from the moveable estate, which is not always the case.

There can be scenarios where such interests or assets are brought back into account for legal rights purposes.

Practitioners should therefore be careful not to assume that just because a deceased does not have legal title or ownership in the strictest sense that they can ignore trusts and gifts entirely. Likewise, when acting for a legal rights claimant, practitioners may want to ascertain if their legal rights entitlements should include any assets in trust or gifted to third parties.

This book will firstly cover the position regarding gifts, before considering assets held in trust structures.

Lifetime gifts excluded for legal rights

The leading case on where gifts are excluded for legal rights purposes is *Allan* v *Stark & Anr*[79], in which Lord Kincairney stated:

> *"I have carefully considered the authorities quoted, and have no doubt that ... it must be regarded as now settled law that the power ... to alienate his movable estate by an inter vivos deed, which wholly divests him of all power over the property disponed, and all benefit from it, is*

[79] *Allan* v *Stark & Anr* (1901) 8 SLT 468.

> *absolute and unqualified, and cannot be regarded as made in fraudem of the rights of his wife merely because it reduces her jus relictae or deprives her of it altogether. A man cannot be held to act fraudulently who does openly what he has a right to do.*"[80]

Therefore, when considering whether gifts are excluded, it requires the following:-

1. the transferor "wholly [divested]" themselves of the asset or rights during their lifetime;

2. the transferor did not retain any benefit from the disposed asset during their lifetime; and

3. the disposition was "absolute and unqualified".

If any of these three criteria are absent, the gift may not meet the test laid down in *Allan* v *Stark* and may require to be brought back into account.

This may mean there are issues where:-

- the gift was made subject to a reservation back to the transferor;

- the transferor did not, in actuality make a gift, and there is a "sham arrangement";

- the gift was invalidly made such that it reverts to the transferor; or

- the circumstances around the transferor were unclear as to whether the intention was to gift or loan the asset / sum in question.

Each of these issues are now covered in further detail, below.

---

[80] Ib id at 469.

Revocable gifts

A revocable gift is one where a party disposes of an asset to another party, but with the ability to revoke the deed of gift, or disposition, such that the asset will return to the transferor.

In these circumstances, the transferor has not wholly divested themselves of the asset as there is power to return the asset or sum to their estate. The question will then be whether the right to revoke the gift passes to the transferor's executors such that they can then revoke the gift and return the asset to the deceased's estate.

In *Hutton's Trs* v. *Hutton's Trs*[81], a husband made a gift to his wife, which was subject to a condition that he had power to revoke it at any time prior to his death. The power to revoke ended on his death and did not transmit to his executors. The court held that because it had not been revoked, the gift effectively crystalised on his death and did not form part of his estate nor consequently part of the legitim fund.

Sham arrangements

Sham arrangements can come in many forms. In Scotland, we don't have the same concept of "sham", as in England, but essentially, it is where an arrangement has been put in place to give an appearance to third parties of a position that is different to the actual legal position[82].

This may crop up when looking at legal rights if an arrangement has been put in place to give the appearance of gifts being made, when, in actuality, the asset has remained in the hands of the transferor throughout their lifetime.

---

[81] *Hutton's Trs* v. *Hutton's Trs* 1916 SC 860.

[82] See the test for Sham in *Snook* v *London & West Riding Investments Ltd* [1967] 2 QB 786 (CA).

This can be seen in *Buchanan* v *Buchanan*[83], in which a father purported to give away almost the entirety of his moveable estate to three children to the exclusion of one black sheep. However, it was done by way of various IOUs that were prepared and then immediately taken back by the father and locked away in a safe to which none of the children had a key and had no access to until after his death.

Lord Ormidale noted:

> "*He may have been entitled to accomplish [defeating legal rights], provided he really did divest absolutely himself in his lifetime. But, looking at the evidence as a jury, I have come to the conclusion that the transaction was a mere bit of acting; that the old man intended to retain control of the money himself, and that his children should not have it till after his death*".[84]

As a result, if any sham arrangements do exist, this would result in the assets or sums gifted forming part of the deceased's moveable estate for legal rights purposes.

Invalid gifts

If gifts were not validly made, then the asset, or in some situations the value of that asset, will be due back to the deceased's estate, and that value would then need to be considered when calculating legal rights. A gift may be deemed invalid where:

- it was made by an attorney or guardian, who did not have power to do so; or
- a claim of incapacity, undue influence, or facility and circumvention is successful.

---

[83] *Buchanan* v *Buchanan* (1876) 3 R 556.

[84] Ib id at 560.

In these circumstances, the gift would be reduced and the asset (or value of the asset, or sale proceeds) would be due back to the deceased's estate and would be included in the legal rights calculation.

This book will not go into the detail of actions for reduction or the grounds for seeking reduction[85]. If any gifts were made by a deceased during their lifetime and there are concerns about validity, advice should be sought.

If an action for reduction is no longer competent, an action for damages or an action for unjustified enrichment may be competent in its place. For any such action, the amount of any sums deemed due to the estate will form part of the legal rights computation.

Gifts deemed to be loans

Another point to be aware of is that an argument could potentially be led that sums apparently gifted were in fact loans. This may be where the circumstances around the transfer are not sufficiently clear as to whether the intention was for the transfer to be an outright gift or if the intention was for the transfer to be a loan, which would be repayable.

If a transfer is, in fact, deemed to have been a loan, then the loan is repayable to the estate and the value would increase any entitlement to legal rights.

There is a general presumption that where sums are transferred it is with the intention these be repaid unless there is clearly an intention for the transfer to be a gift or "donation"[86].

If there were any transfers made by a deceased where there was no clear evidence that the intention was for such a transfer to be a gift, the

---

[85] For the test for undue influence, see *Gray* v *Binny* (1879) 7 R 332, for the test for facility and circumvention see *Mackay* v *Campbell* 1967 SC (HL).

[86] See British Linen Co. v Martin, &c (1849) 11 D. 1004.

executors of the deceased can seek repayment of that sum or asset and recover it to the deceased's estate. In those circumstances, the value of the asset, or sum repaid, would be an asset of the estate and would increase the entitlement to legal rights.

There is some dubiety as to whether gifts from a parent to a child have the same presumption against donation, or whether such gifts would be deemed to be *ex pietate*, in other words for the usual love and affection they have for their child. The case law and dicta on this is not definitive.

In *Malcolm* v *Campbell*[87], the circumstances were that a payment was made from a father to a daughter on her marriage and it was held that the presumption against donation did not apply in this situation. In the dicta, Lord Lee commented:

> "*...donation is not presumed, but where the person said to have made it is under a natural obligation to provide for the person to whom it is said to be made there is no onus on the person receiving. The presumption rather is that it may have been a gift* ex pietate*...*[88]"

The key issue with the dicta noted above is that it states "it may have been" which is not definitive, and, as such, will still rely on the facts and circumstances as to whether the transfer was a gift *ex pietate.*

In this case, the gift on marriage had the quality of a donation, but an argument led was that the sum transferred was too excessive to be considered a gift. The Lord Justice-Clerk commented that the excessive nature did not change the fact that it was, in his opinion, a gift[89].

---

[87] *Malcolm* v *Campbell* (1899) 17 R 255.

[88] Ib id, at 257.

[89] "*I do not consider it to be made out that there was any such extravagant disproportion between this sum and his other means as to exclude the idea of a gift*" per Lord Justice Clerk at 258.

More recently, Perth Sheriff Court heard the case of *Mailer* v *Mailer*[90] , in which it was suggested that a payment made by a mother "*so that she could help her son in an hour of need… [and acted] out of a sense of natural obligation*" was also to be considered a gift, rather than a loan.

As such, it is not clear-cut where the payment has been made from parent to child and it will be dependent on the facts and circumstances.

The key point to take away from this chapter is that if a presumption of loan can or might apply, it may increase the legal rights fund. Practitioners ought to consider the likelihood of success in these scenarios, whether acting for executors or a legal rights claimant, and advise accordingly.

Entitlement to trusts

Another scenario that crops up in practice is where a deceased had an interest in a trust. Practitioners should not assume that because assets are held in a trust structure that they are excluded from a legal rights calculation. It will very much depend on the type of trust and the facts and circumstances as to what is or what might be included in a legal rights calculation.

Interests may be held in:

- a bare trust
- a liferent trust, or
- a discretionary trust

Different rules apply to each, which are covered below.

---

[90] *Mailer* v *Mailer* [2019] SCPER101.

Bare trusts

If the deceased had an entitlement to a bare trust, this means that they were absolutely entitled to the capital and income and could, at any time, demand the assets be transferred to them.

In *Drysdale's Trustees* v *Drysdale*[91], Lord Fleming noted:

> *"There are two propositions with regard to legitim which require to be borne in mind in considering this case. The first is that legitim is payable out of the moveable estate belonging to the deceased at the date of his death, and in applying this proposition regard must be had to the beneficial right rather than to formal title. If property is vested in trustees but belongs beneficially to the deceased person at the date of his death, it is subject to claims of legitim.*
>
> *... I am of opinion that (irrespective of the special provision) the truster here all along retained a right to the funds settled in the trust deed."*[92]

As such any assets held in a bare trust ought to be treated as belonging to the deceased for the purposes of calculating legal rights. Whether the underlying assets are included in the moveable estate will depend on whether they are treated as moveable or heritable. Chapter 8 discusses the concept of conversion in more detail.

Liferent trusts

It will depend on whether the deceased was the income or capital beneficiary of the trust as to what is included, or excluded, for legal rights purposes.

---

[91] *Drysdale's Trustees* v *Drysdale* 1940 SLT 101.

[92] Ib id at 107.

Entitlement to income

If the deceased had a liferent interest in a trust, in other words they were entitled to the income of the trust, they are entitled to the use and enjoyment of the trust capital, or the net free income earned on that capital.

An income entitlement ends on death, so there is no continuing entitlement. There may be a sum of income due up until the deceased's date of death, which the trustees ought to quantify, and this would be included in a legal rights calculation.

This often occurs where income is not paid, direct, to the liferenter but is collected by the trustees and paid to the liferent beneficiary at specified times throughout the year or annually.

For example, if a liferent trust holds a holiday home and rental income is collected by the trustees, and paid to the liferenter in March and September. If the liferenter dies in July, there may be income earned between March and July held that is due to be paid to the liferenter. That sum will form part of the deceased's net moveable estate.

In this scenario, the deceased has no entitlement to the capital of the liferent trust. Depending on how and when the liferent trust was set up, the underlying capital may be added to the estate for inheritance tax purposes, but the capital is excluded for the purposes of legal rights calculations.

Because the capital of a liferent trust described above is excluded from a legal rights calculation, an option for clients looking to avoid legal rights may be to create a lifetime liferent trust, in which they give themselves the entitlement to the income, but the capital is held for other named beneficiaries or on discretionary terms[93].

---

[93] There may be tax implications to creating such a trust and any clients ought to be properly advised on the consequences before proceeding.

Collie v. *Pirie's Trustees*[94], was such a case where a transfer of property was made with an express reservation of a liferent and the court deemed this to be effective.

Entitlement to capital

If a deceased has an entitlement (or potential entitlement) to the capital of a liferent trust, this means that the trustees of the liferent trust will hold that capital until the liferent comes to an end – either because the liferenter dies, renounces their liferent or the liferent fails for some other reason[95].

If the deceased does have a potential interest in the capital, but the liferent trust is ongoing, it will depend on whether they have vest in that capital interest or not.

The terms of the trust deed ought to be considered, and there will be two potential outcomes:-

- if vesting is delayed until the liferent is terminated, then the deceased will not have survived to take a vested interest in the trust, and it can be ignored; or

- if the deceased had vest in the capital, then for IHT purposes they are said to have a reversionary interest ("excluded property" for IHT purposes[96]).

Some authors have suggested that because a deceased has to hold estate at the time of their death for it to be included in legal rights calculations, that certain reversionary interests may be excluded[97].

---

[94] *Collie* v. *Pirie's Trustees* (1856) 13 D 506.

[95] This book will not cover the intricacies of when a liferent comes to an end.

[96] s48 Inheritance Tax Act 1984.

[97] See *The Laws of Scotland: Stair Memorial Encyclopaedia,* Vol 25, para 784.

That said, if vesting is absolute and a deceased can be said to have the beneficial interest in the capital at the time of death, albeit postponed until a liferent comes to an end, it may be argued that this ought to form part of a legal rights claim.

As with bare trusts, whether the underlying assets form part of the legal rights calculation would then depend on whether they are treated as moveable or heritable, which is covered in later chapters.

Discretionary trusts

For discretionary trusts, the general rule is that a beneficiary has no fixed interest in the trust and therefore there is no value or interest to include in their estate.

Some practitioners do use trusts as a vehicle to avoid legal rights claims against estates and they can be effective for this purpose.

There are a few of scenarios where this may not be the case:

- trusts in which the truster or settlor (hereafter "settlor") have retained an interest
- trusts with a radical right to revert to settlor
- trusts with default beneficiaries

<u>Settlor interested trusts</u>

The first scenario is in relation to certain settlor interested trusts. It will depend on the construction of the trust deed and the facts and circumstances, but there is a suggestion that interests in such trusts ought to be included in calculations for legal rights.

Professor Meston opined that the fact the settlor is a beneficiary of the trust means that the assets of the trust still form part of their estate for legal rights purposes[98]. This opinion was based on the case law relating to gifts, dealt with earlier in this chapter[99], and that a settlor has not completely divested himself of the asset and all rights to it.

If a client is therefore looking to avoid legal rights claims by creating a discretionary trust and naming themselves as a potential beneficiary, practitioners should take care to highlight the various case law where this has failed to defeat legal rights[100].

The key appears to be whether there has been sufficient divesting of an interest in the property.

In *Rowley* v *Rowley*[101], Mr Rowley set up a trust and formally transferred shares in his company to the trustees. After his death, his wife claimed legal rights and argued that the shares should still form part of the calculation on the basis that her husband had retained an interest.

The argument was made on the basis that no dividends were paid on the shareholdings. This was because the husband took a salary that exhausted excess profits and so no dividends could be paid. It was therefore argued that he had continued to enjoy the income from those shares and had not divested himself fully of the shares.

The court, however, disagreed, as there was an irrevocable transfer and his salary was from the company, not the shares.

In *Campbell* v *Campbell's Trustees*[102] there was a potential reversion to the truster, but because this did not materialise, the assets in the trust were excluded for legal rights purposes. This case also included useful dicta

---

[98] Opinion 49, Professor M. C. Meston, *Meston's Succession Opinions* W. Green / Sweet & Maxwell 2000.

[99] See *Allan* v *Stark* op cit.

[100] see *Lyon's Trs* v *Miller* (1903) 5 F 1096; *Little* v *Little* (1856) 18 D 701 and *Craigie* v *Craigie* 1811 Hume 288.

[101] *Rowley* v *Rowley* (1917) SLT 16.

[102] *Campbell* v *Campbell's Trustees* 1967 SLT (Notes) 30.

that by appointing the truster as a trustee, this did not impact on whether the assets were sufficiently divested:

> "*While I can see that the appointment of the truster as a trustee might give rise in certain circumstances to difficulties in trust administration, in my opinion the divestiture is no less complete and the deed no less irrevocable where the truster is a trustee than where all the trustees are 'independent persons'.*"[103]

As such, simply creating a trust and transferring assets to the trust where the settlor is a beneficiary may not be enough for legal rights purposes and, of course, there are various tax implications to consider too when advising clients of trusts.

If a client is looking to reduce a claim to legal rights on their estate, one option that could be considered is a loan trust. A discretionary trust could be created, excluding the settlor as a beneficiary, but appointing the settlor as a trustee[104]. The settlor would then make a valid gift to the trust, wholly divesting themselves of the asset or sum. The trustees could then loan the sum back to the settlor (assuming sufficient power is given to do so). The settlor would then hold the assets or sum in question, but owe a debt to the trust. That debt would be deductible in calculating legal rights and reduce the value of any legal rights claim, accordingly[105].

Whilst this structure appears to get around the existing case law, until it is tested by a court any risks should be stressed to clients that such trusts may be subject to challenge and might fail before proceeding. All

---

[103] Ib id, per Lord Thomson at 31.

[104] Which per Lord Thomson, ib id, is not in itself a reason to bring the trust fund within the remit of legal rights.

[105] There would be Inheritance Tax considerations and dangers of this approach, in particular the loan would likely be caught by s103 of the Finance Act 1986 and would not be a deductible debt for IHT purposes, which may trigger a double-IHT charge, careful planning would therefore need considered.

procedural steps in setting up the trust and delivering assets to the trustees also ought to be followed to ensure there is less chance of a challenge.

Radical right

The other scenario that may crop up in practice is where the settlor has a radical right in the trust, which essentially means that the trust property reverts to the settlor for one reason or another.

It may be because a trust was not validly constituted, for example if a settlor is later deemed to have done so under undue influence, where a trust was created by an attorney who did not have sufficient powers to do so, or there may have been some flaw or error in the creation of the trust itself.

Likewise, there may be a scenario where all other beneficiaries predeceased the settlor, and provision as to what happens to the trust property has not been made, such that the assets revert to the settlor.

In these scenarios, any assets held by the trustees are then treated as being held on bare trust for the settlor and the position set out in *Drysdale's Trustees* v *Drysdale*[106] applies.

That case dealt with a scenario where there was a radical right: if other beneficiaries predeceased, there was a direction for the trust to pass to the parties under the settlor's Will.

Lord Fleming noted:

> *"... I am of opinion that (irrespective of the special provision) the truster here all along retained a right to the funds settled in the trust deed...*
>
> *the truster in effect reserved to himself power to deal by testamentary disposition with any shares which lapsed under the forfeiture clause. In other words, the forfeited shares really devolve under the truster's*

---

[106] *Drysdale's Trustees* v *Drysdale* 1940 SLT 101.

> *testamentary disposition, and if this be so, they are necessarily subject to the claims for legitim, because, in accordance with the proposition above set forth, legitim cannot be diminished by a testamentary settlement."*[107]

The assets in the trust were therefore deemed to form part of the legal rights claim, regardless of the fact the default position was for it to pass to beneficiaries named under his Will, as this was seen as giving the settlor the right to divest of those assets in a testamentary manner.

This can be distinguished from the case of *Campbell* v *Campbell's Trustees*[108] mentioned earlier on the basis that the potential reversion to the truster in that case did not materialise.

Practitioners may also come across radical rights when dealing with pro forma trust deeds.

> Example
>
> A pro forma trust deed included a box where trustees are to be named (in order to appoint trustees). If no names are completed, there may not be a valid trust without trustees. Even if the form was signed purporting to assign the life policy to the trustees, in the absence of appointed trustees to take delivery of the assets purportedly being assigned, there would not be a valid trust and the policy would revert to the settlor's estate.

Practitioners should take care when acting for clients where legal rights will be a key issue in their succession planning and the client advises they have set up such a trust. It would be prudent in such circumstances, to request copies of any trust paperwork or pro forma deeds to check that procedures were followed properly to avoid surprises after a death.

---

107 Ib id, per Lord Fleming at 107.

108 *Campbell* v *Campbell's Trustees* 1967 SLT (Notes) 30.

Defeasible interest

Another scenario is where discretionary trusts are created, in which default beneficiaries are stipulated.

> Example
>
> A trust deed states that in the event no appointments are made within five years of a date of death, the trust is to be divided 50/50 between A and B. In that scenario, A has a 50% interest in the trust, which is a called a "defeasible interest". A is therefore entitled to 50% of that trust until and unless the trustees make an appointment otherwise.

If a person dies having a defeasible interest in a trust, at their date of death, arguably, the deceased does have beneficial ownership and it could form part of a legal rights calculation. The facts and circumstances of the case will prevail as to whether that share would have any value or not

Often it may be necessarily to have the value of any defeasible interest actuarially valued to take into account likelihood of certain parties surviving and the valuation of the sums potentially due.

This is a complex area and if it does come up in practice, practitioners should take care to seek advice on any issues of including the value in the estate for not just legal rights purposes, but for inheritance tax purposes.

CHAPTER SEVEN

WHEN IS "HERITABLE" "MOVEABLE"?

What is heritable property?

Having said a person's moveable estate is anything that is not "heritable", one has to consider what is heritable[109].

A heritable right is a "real right" under the law of Scotland, i.e. it is a right over land, rather than being a personal right against a person or individuals.

This includes a registered title in land and buildings, which is held in the name of the deceased and not held as part of a partnership or business interest (see Chapter 9).

Whilst broadly speaking any registered real right will be treated as heritable, that may not always be the case for legal rights purposes. This chapter will highlight scenarios where that general position can be displaced.

Foreign property

As noted in an earlier Chapter, the worldwide net moveable estate is used to calculate legal rights. If a deceased owned property outside of Scotland, practitioners will therefore need to ascertain whether that property is considered heritable (and therefore excluded from the calculation) or if it

---

109 Practitioners may be aware that there is no specific definition for "heritable property", and the Scottish Law Commission did not use the term in the Report on the Abolition of the Feudal System (Scot Law Com No 168) 1999, so the term is merely understood to be real or immoveable property.

is considered as moveable (and the value is therefore included in a calculation).

The law as to what is heritable or moveable will vary from jurisdiction to jurisdiction and what is classed as heritable in Scotland, may be treated as moveable in another jurisdiction and vice versa.

The general position is that if the asset is of a character that would be classed as heritable if it were situated in Scotland, then it should be treated as heritable and excluded for legal rights purposes.

In some jurisdictions assets that appear heritable in nature convert to moveable property under their succession laws. That said, there is authority that any conversion applied in foreign jurisdictions is ignored, and executors should look to the nature of the underlying asset and ignore any conversion.

In *Macdonald* v *Macdonald's Executrix*[110] land in Canada was owned by a deceased. Under Canadian succession law, the land was treated as moveable in terms of those parties entitled to inherit it. The question raised was whether the fact Canadian succession law treated that land as moveable in Canada would affect the nature of the land for legal rights purposes.

However, it was held by Lord Thankerton that:

> *"Any fictional element of moveability which is attached to it for the purpose of identifying the persons entitled to succeed to it is incidental to determination of the rights of succession to land in the foreign country, and does not affect its character as immoveable…."*[111]

---

[110] *Macdonald* v *Macdonald's Executrix* 1932 SLT 381.

[111] Ib id at 386.

As a result, the fact that Canadian succession laws treated the land as moveable for succession purposes was irrelevant and did not affect the character of the asset, which was immovable or heritable.

The key is therefore to consider whether the asset is of a character that is heritable (excluded from legal rights) or moveable (included), using the same tests as we would in Scotland and ignoring any legal fictions applied in the relevant jurisdiction.

Heritable rights deemed to be moveable

There are certain scenarios where interests or rights may appear on the face of it to be heritable, because they relate to land and buildings that have a registered title, but interest or right is treated as moveable.

These scenarios arise with:-

- there is a right attached to the heritable property, but exercising the right, or the value of the right is moveable – discussed below
- the registered title doesn't reflect the ownership – discussed below
- the property is treated as moveable as a result of "conversion" – discussed in chapter 8
- the property is used in a partnership and is treated as partnership property, which means the deceased has a moveable interest in it – discussed in chapter 9

Baronies

Baronies and other dignities of office are honorary titles, for example "Lord", "Earl" or "Baron". Historically, these were heritable in nature and attached to the title deeds and a person would inherit the title when they inherited the land it was attached to and took title to the land.

Following the enactment of the Abolition of Feudal Tenure etc. (Scotland) Act 2000, baronies are no longer attached to the title deeds, instead:

> "...on and after the appointed day any such dignity shall be, and shall be transferable only as, incorporeal heritable property (and shall not be a right as respects which a deed can be registered in the Land Register of Scotland or recorded in the Register of Sasines)..."[112]

As such, baronies are still treated as heritable, albeit incorporeal assets. Issues may arise if a barony has not transferred from party, A, to another, B, in which case party B may only be said to have a personal right to the barony and not the right in the heritable incorporeal.

Baronies (and other titles) can be bought and sold and there is market for these and, as such, they do have a value.

Some landed estates may include historic baronies that were once attached to the land, but over time they were not specifically referred to in the title deeds. As such, when dealing with these historic landed estates, or estates where there have been titles, care should be taken to ascertain whether there are any such baronies or titles that the deceased was entitled to and whether the interest is that of a heritable incorporeal asset or a right to have the barony transferred.

<u>Minerals</u>

If the deceased had an entitlement to minerals, these may be moveable in nature depending on whether the interest is held separate to the land. A conveyancer will be able to check this for you and advise. If they are moveable, a value ought to be placed on those mineral rights for legal rights purposes.

---

[112] s63(2) Abolition of Feudal Tenure etc. (Scotland) Act 2000.

Pre-emption rights

Some title deeds include a pre-emption right in favour of the deceased, which will also pass to their executors. That pre-emption right may have a value to it, depending on whether the right can still be relied upon and how the pre-emption operates.

A conveyancer will be able to confirm whether the pre-emption right still stands after the Abolition of Feudal Tenure etc. (Scotland) Act 2000. If the pre-emption right was created before 28 November 2004, and it (1) does not concern maintenance obligations, (2) was not a feudal burden, and (3) the benefitted property is sufficiently identified, the pre-emption right may stand.

If the pre-emption does transmit to the executors of the deceased, then practitioners should consider whether the potential exercising of that right has a value that is distinct from the heritable land owned.

For example, in farming estates there may have been cottages sold to farm employees, but with a pre-emption in favour of the original farming estate to purchase it back at a later date. As selling the farm as a whole with those cottages may be more valuable than selling with potential gaps in the farming estate, the pre-emption right can add a value to the estate.

Such pre-emption rights don't entitle the executors to the underlying, registered, land and buildings, but there is added value in being able to exercise the right, which is moveable in nature.

Reinstatement rights

Where heritable property has been damaged (e.g. by fire or flood), there is often a right for the property to be reinstated under an insurance policy (assuming there are no special factors that render the policy invalid).

Where the reinstatement has not been carried out (or not carried out in full at the time of death), there will be two distinct assets, each with a value:-

1) the heritable property, which may have a nil or minimal value due to the damage, and

2) the right under the insurance policy to have the property reinstated, i.e. the reinstatement right.

The value to be placed on the reinstatement right will depend on the value of the claim (or the value outstanding at the date of death if partially paid prior to death).

Although the right to reinstate is attached to that specific heritable property, the value of that claim is moveable in nature as the right is to receive a cash equivalent from the insurer.

For example, if a person dies and, at the time of their death, they own a house, which has been damaged by fire. The heritable property, being the derelict house, is valued at only £80,000. There will be a separate asset of the estate, being the insurance policy claim, so if it costs £100,000 to reinstate the property to its previous condition, that £100,000 is treated as a moveable asset.

It is irrelevant that the expenditure is spent on the heritable asset or that the value will be reflected in the sale price of the house.

Title deeds do not reflect ownership

There can be scenarios where an interest in heritable property could be deemed moveable because of how title is held.

In England, there are the concepts of legal ownership and the beneficial interest. The legal ownership would be the person(s) with the registered title, but such title may be held as bare trustee for parties who have a beneficial interest in the property.

Whilst we don't have the same concept of beneficial ownership for heritable property in Scotland, we do have scenarios where the person named in the relevant register is just holding title as bare trustee and nominee for one or more underlying parties.

Examples include:

- The registered title holder is a parent or guardian for a minor child who cannot hold title in the Land Register;

- Title was registered in the name of a title holder, who has since married or started to cohabit and they signed a deed of gift and declaration of trust in favour of their partner to gift a share of the property to their partner, but no formal conveyance was undertaken;

- Title is registered in the name of a deceased or in the trustees of a trust, but the executors or trustees have appropriated or appointed the interest in the property to a beneficiary, such that the beneficiary has a vested interest in the heritable property; or

- Title is registered in the name of a sole surviving party as a result of a survivorship destination, but the survivorship destination was evacuated by a minute of agreement, which is not registered in a land register, such that the sole surviving party holds the registered title, but the executors of the deceased has a right to a share.

Each of these scenarios are comparable with the English concept of beneficial ownership as there is a registered title holder, who is effectively holding that title as bare trustee, only. The implications of bare trusts were discussed earlier in chapter 6.

The party who has an interest in that bare trust, has a personal right against the registered title holder to formally convey the asset to them, but they do not have a right in the underlying heritable property itself. This can be seen in *Fleming's Trustee* v *Fleming*[113].

In this case, a survivorship destination was evacuated by an inter vivos deed. A Trustee in Sequestration was appointed to administer [Mr Fleming's] estate, but he did not seek to convert that personal right into

---

113 *Fleming's Trustee* v *Fleming* 2000 SC 206.

a real right (i.e. he did not seek to have the registered title updated to reflect that ownership). Therefore, upon the death of the bankrupt party, the property passed to the survivor, who became the sole registered title holder. The court held that the Trustee in Bankruptcy did not have a real right in the heritable property, but had a personal right against the survivor for the value of the half share of the property.

As such any entitlement to a heritable property where title is held in this manner could, potentially, form part of a legal rights calculation, subject to the principles of conversion, which is discussed in the next chapter.

Evacuations of Survivorship Destinations

Survivorship destinations and documents that purport to evacuate survivorship destinations have been much debated by both property and private client practitioners for some time now[114]. If a document evacuating the survivorship destination is registered in a property register, such that it formally amends the heritable title and the parties become the registered title holders, this will put the matter beyond doubt.

Unfortunately, as this may trigger a first registration into the Land Register, many clients wish to avoid those costs and will instead register an Evacuation Agreement in the Books of Council and Session or in the General Register of Sasines under Miscellaneous Deeds.

There is no clear authority on how these are treated for legal rights purposes.

It appears to be accepted by practitioners that the executors do have a personal right under such an agreement, which right would entitle the executors to seek to have the 50% share of the property conveyed to the estate by the other party in implementation of such an agreement, or, failing that, an action for damages for a half share of the value. However,

---

[114] See: "Contentious executries: problems with succession to heritable property", Roddy MacLeod, SLT 2016, 13, 61-63, "Survivorship destinations – the debate continues", John Kerrigan, SLT 2014, 37, 175-178.

whether that is heritable or moveable for legal rights purposes is ambiguous.

This author is aware of arguments having been led that as the right is to have the heritable property conveyed, the estate has a heritable interest for the purposes of legal rights (and ought to be excluded) referring to the principles of conversion (discussed in the next chapter). This relies on the fact that the estate is entitled to the heritable property, so it would only become a moveable interest (under conversion) if and when the property was not conveyed, but an equivalent value or damages paid.

That said, many practitioners will argue the opposite that as it is a personal right, only, as it is not a real right and is therefore moveable. This may be a stronger argument on the basis that there was an opportunity by the deceased, in life, to convert their interest to a real right, but perhaps chose not do so. Certainly, in the *Flemings* case[115], it was noted that "it is for the disponee to protect his own title"[116], so if rights are not converted in life, it may be difficult to assert they ought to be treated as real or heritable after a death.

Until there is a decision by the court to put this matter beyond doubt, it appears likely that practitioners will require to advise executors and beneficiaries of the potential that such entitlements may be treated as moveable.

---

115 *Fleming's Trustee* v *Fleming* 2000 SC 206.

116 Ib id, per Lord Caplan at 216.

CHAPTER EIGHT

CONVERSION

What is conversion?

Conversion is where a right in heritable property is made moveable and vice versa by some act of the deceased. This may be where the deceased:

- Entered into a contract for sale / purchase prior to death;
- Was entitled to a heritable property as a beneficiary of an estate and title was not transferred prior to death or;
- stipulated in their will that heritable property ought to be bought / sold.

In these circumstances, conversion may apply to make what is otherwise a heritable property "moveable" for the purposes of legal rights, or vice versa.

Conversion can generally fall into two categories, actual conversion (contracts for sale / purchase) or constructive conversion.

Actual conversion

Contracts for sale

The simplest form of conversion can be seen where the deceased owned a heritable property prior to their death, but had entered into a binding contract for its sale. If the conveyance has not taken place, the deceased will still hold a registered real right in the property, but it will be subject to that contract.

This has been held to be moveable property, since all the deceased is entitled to is the cash sum payable under that contract, or if it was partially paid before death, the balance due.

In *Chiesley* v *His Sisters*[117], the deceased had entered into a Minute to dispone lands, had received part of the purchase price, and the remainder of the purchase price was held by the purchaser at the time of death. The sum held by the purchaser and still due was held to be moveable.

Involuntary contracts for sale

Conversion will still apply even where the sale was not voluntarily entered into by the deceased, as can be seen in:

- *Heron* v *Espie*[118] which was as a result of a compulsory purchase;
- *Macfarlane* v *Greig*[119] which was as a result of an action of division and sale; and
- *Howden Petr*[120], which was on the sale by a bondholder.

Purchases prior to death

If a purchase of heritable property is completed prior to death, but a registered titled has not yet been obtained, then this will have the reverse effect and will convert moveable estate to heritable[121], and the purchase price will be the value, which can be excluded for legal rights purposes.

---

117 *Chiesley* v *His Sisters* (1704) Mor 5531.

118 *Heron* v *Espie* (1856) 18 D 917.

119 *Macfarlane* v *Greig* (1895) 22 R. 405.

120 *Howden Petr* 1910 2 SLT 250.

121 See: *Ramsay* v *Ramsay* (1887) 15 R 25; *Fairlie's Trustees* v *Fairlie's Curator Bonis* 1932 SC 216.

<u>Contracts with suspensive conditions</u>

Practitioners should, however, take care where a sale or purchase was subject to suspensive conditions as it will depend on whether the condition had purified at the date of death as to whether conversion occurs. In *McArthurs Executors* v *Guild*[122], the Lord President noted:

> "*...if a certain condition were purified he would be bound to sell the subject, but at the moment no one could know whether the condition would be purified. I think the condition was purely suspensive.*[123]"

This case was in relation to the ademption of a legacy, but the principle was that without purification of the condition, the interest remained heritable as the deceased was not bound by the contract at the time of death.

Constructive conversion

<u>Deceased entitled as a beneficiary</u>

Conversion may also apply where a deceased has an interest in a trust or in another estate, which includes heritable property.

For example, a testator leaves a legacy of a heritable property to A. If A dies before receiving that legacy, does conversion apply so as to make his interest moveable in nature?

The leading case on this is the House of Lord case *Buchanan* v *Angus, &c*[124], in which Lord Westbury explained the position as follows:

> *"Conversion was a question of intention, and depended on the nature and effect of the directions given in any settlement or will. If real or*

---

[122] *McArthurs Executors* v *Guild* [1908] SLR 551.

[123] Ib id, per the Lord President at 553.

[124] *Buchanan* v *Angus, &c* (1862) 24 D (HL) 5.

> *heritable property were vested in trustees upon an absolute and unconditional trust for sale, either declared or necessarily implied, and the proceeds of such sale were disposed of, there was an out-and-out conversion for the purposes of that disposition; and the interest of every beneficiary taken under the disposition was of the nature of personal or moveable property.*
>
> *"But if, instead of an absolute and unqualified trust or direction for sale, the right to sell was made to depend on the discretion or will of the trustees; or was to arise only in case of necessity; or was limited to particular purposes… "indispensable to the execution of the trust," then, in any of these cases, until the discretion was exercised, or the necessity arose, and was acted on, …there was no change in the quality of the property; and the heritable estate must continue to be held and transmitted as heritable."*[125]

As conversion looks at what interest the beneficiary has in the property, it will very much depend on the facts and circumstances of each case, and it is not always straightforward. Much of the case law relates to the ademption of legacies, rather than to the treatment of an interest for legal rights purposes. That said, applying the principles in *Buchanan*,[126] above, to the scenario above, A would appear to have a heritable interest in the legacy if it is clear that the sale is not necessary or required (e.g. for abatement purposes).

Conversion by will

Following *Buchanan* v *Angus*, constructive conversion applies to the interests that beneficiaries take under a will. It is unclear, however, whether constructive conversion has the effect of converting heritable property to moveable for the purposes of legal rights claimants.

There appears to be conflicting authority on this within The Laws of Scotland: Stair Memorial Encyclopaedia ("Stair"). Stair suggests that an

---

[125] Ib id, per Lord Westbury at 6.

[126] Ib id.

absolute direction to sell heritable property under a will would have the effect of converting it to moveable and that heritable property would therefore form part of the legal rights calculation[127]. However, Stair also states that conversion may apply from moveable to heritable by an act of will, but not from heritable to moveable[128].

Certain authors have cited Stair as authority for the proposition that conversion does apply to increase the legal rights fund[129]. Whereas other authors suggested that conversion would not apply in this manner for legal rights purposes[130].

The judicial authority remains that legal rights are calculated by "valuing the moveable estate left by the [deceased]"[131]. If the deceased left heritable property at the date of death, it would only be included in that calculation if a legal fiction were applied to it to suggest that it was moveable.

At the time of writing, there appears to be no judicial authority confirming whether a direction in a Will could result in heritable property being made moveable for the purpose of legal rights.

There is, however, authority that moveable property would not convert to heritable under a direction in a will, so as to avoid legal rights, and such a direction would only impact on the interest beneficiaries of the estate receive[132]. Arguably, this is authority that the converse also ought to be true. However, the court may have taken this position as a matter of public policy.

---

127 *The Laws of Scotland: Stair Memorial Encyclopaedia,* Vol 25, para 816.

128 Ib id, Vol 18, para 14.

129 See: Hilary Hiram, *The Scots Law of Succession*, 2nd edition, at 2.40.

130 Alan Barr et al "*Drafting Wills in Scotland*" (Second Edition) para 6.35.

131 *Selsdon* v *Selsdon* 1934 SC (HL) 24, per Lord Thankerton at 31.

132 *Naismith* v *Boyes* (1899) 1 F (HL) 79.

In *Hogg* v *Hamilton*[133], Lord Deas commented that his view is:

> *"If at the date of the truster's death the estate is heritable in its nature the words used as to what is to be done with those subjects are, I think, to be construed with a presumption in favour of keeping them in their then existing form rather than of changing them into personalty."*[134]

There is also the concept of reconversion, which applies where there is an express direction in the Will, but a beneficiary opts to do the opposite. However, given the implications of conversion in the first place are uncertain, this book will not go into the possible ramifications of reconversion further.

In the absence of judicial authority, it is difficult to say with any certainty what the correct treatment of conversion or reconversion is.

In practice, if advising executors where this issue crops up, specialist advice should be taken, and some options may be to:-

- Seek counsel's opinion – to avoid obtaining multiple differing views, parties may wish to agree to jointly instruct counsel and agree to be bound by that opinion;

- Seek rectification of the will[135] – for example, if it is clear there has been a drafting error and there was no intention to increase the legal rights funds in this manner (extrinsic evidence is permitted[136] and so if the testator was clearly wishing to avoid or minimise exposure to legal rights, such evidence could be led);

- Seek agreement – as executors owe the duty to the residuary beneficiaries and there is no clear authority on whether the legal

133 *Hogg* v *Hamilton* (1877) 4 R 845 .

134 Ib id at 850.

135 s3 Succession (Scotland) Act 2016, for deaths on or after 1 November 2016.

136 Ib id s3(3).

rights fund should be inflated by the heritable property or not, executors may wish to protect their position by seeking agreement from all parties before distributing the estate or agreeing a legal rights calculation (parties may prefer this route to the more costly court options); or

- Seek directions from court – if agreement cannot be reached, executors may wish to resort to the court for directions on the proper distribution of the estate.

The key lesson to learn is that when drafting a Will, careful instructions should be sought before including any clause where there is a direction to sell. If a client wants to include it in their Will to ensure that they are made aware of the potential impact it may have for legal rights purposes.

CHAPTER NINE

PARTNERSHIP PROPERTY

Basic principles

It is settled law that if a person dies with an interest in a partnership, what the deceased holds is an interest in that partnership, not any specific assets, and that interest requires to be valued for the purposes of legal rights in light of the value of the business as a whole.

The general position is that an interest in a partnership will be moveable, regardless of what the underlying assets are within that partnership.

s22 of the Partnership Act 1890 states:

"Where land or any heritable interest therein has become partnership property, it shall, unless the contrary intention appears, be treated as between the partners (including the representatives of a deceased partner), and also as between the heirs of a deceased partner and his executors or administrators, as personal or moveable and not real or heritable estate."

The key point to highlight is that although the default position is for heritable property to form part of the business and be treated as moveable, there is scope to argue otherwise, as made clear in the legislation.

The key questions are therefore:

- Can s22 be disapplied if a contrary intention is shown; or
- Should s22 be disapplied because it can be shown the property does not form part of the partnership?

Can s22 be dis-applied?

Some partnership agreements may attempt to alter the general position by inverting the use of the words "heritable" and "moveable", for example:

"Any land or any heritable interest in land which becomes partnership property will be treated as between the partners (including the representatives of a deceased partner) and also as between the heirs of a deceased partner and his executors or administrators as real or heritable estate and not as personal or moveable estate and Section 22 of the Partnership Act 1890 shall not apply"

The key words in these types of clauses are "as between the partners". This is because it will be an agreement between the partners who are parties to the deed. A person can also bind their executors, with such wording, but it would be difficult to bind somebody who is not party to the original contract to agree to that position, in particular heirs of an estate, or legal rights claimants. That said, it would be for a legal rights claimant to argue the point in practice and there appears no judicial authority on the effectiveness of such clauses in a legal rights scenario. That said, it may show a contrary intention to s22 if put to that test.

Is the property "partnership property" or not?

The second question is whether heritable property is actually owned by the partnership and forms part of the business, meaning s22 applies, or alternatively, if the asset is owned by an individual or individuals as heritable property, which is merely used by the partnership.

This distinction can determine whether heritable property is included in the legal rights calculation or not.

This is a question not just confined to the law on legal rights, but often arises in relation to determining whether business property relief applies, or in the context of family law, so the relevant case law is not specific to legal rights, and it may be necessary to look to some other decisions.

s20 of the Partnership Act[137] provides some further guidance on what is partnership property, as follows:

"[it] must be held and applied by the partners exclusively for the purposes of the partnership, and in accordance with the partnership agreement[138]".

The legislation further states that:

"Unless the contrary intention appears, property bought with money belonging to the firm is deemed to have been bought on account of the firm."[139]

The legislation also confirms that any profits derived from non-partnership property are used to buy additional land or estate, such additions will also not be partnership property, but will be held as co-owners "in the absence of an agreement to the contrary".[140]

Careful analysis will therefore be required to ascertain whether property is indeed partnership property or not.

In *Jack* v *Jack*[141], Lord Drummond Young noted:

> *"It is important to note that section 20 does not of itself render property partnership property. Before any property becomes partnership property, one of the conditions in subsection (1) must be satisfied: either the property must be brought into the partnership stock, or the property must be acquired on account of the firm, or for the purposes and in the course of its business. The reason for those requirements is obvious: partnership property must be distinguished from an individual partner's own property, and consequently something is required to*

---

[137] Partnership Act 1890.

[138] Ib id, s20(1).

[139] Ib id, s21.

[140] Ib id s20(3).

[141] *Jack* v *Jack* 2016 Fam LR 177.

establish that the property is truly the property of the partnership rather than part of the personal estate of an individual partner…"[142]

Determining whether property is "partnership property"

In order to determine whether the asset is held by the partnership or not, it is necessary to consider various evidence, which may include reviewing:

- Any partnership agreement
- Titles to the land and buildings
- Business accounts
- Source of funds for the purchase of the property
- Tax Returns
- Business records

None of the evidence can be looked at in isolation and it will be necessary to consider everything together to ascertain the intention of the parties as to whether the land and buildings were intended to be "partnership property".

Whilst some of the evidence may be held to be a strong indication of intention, for example including a farm on a balance sheet, this must be looked at in the round and extrinsic evidence will be considered.

Partnership Agreement

The first place to look is probably in a partnership agreement, if there is one, to see whether it includes any provisions on the heritable property.

---

[142] Ib id at 181.

Some agreements will specify what capital is held, by whom and how it is used in a schedule showing the capital or heritage account. Others may include clauses like the one mentioned above.

That said, even if a partnership agreement does appear to exclude heritable property from the business, that is not the only source of evidence one must look at.

s19 of the Partnership Act 1890 allows for variations of a partnership agreement by the acting and acquiescence of the parties:

> "The mutual rights and duties of partners, whether ascertained by agreement or defined by this Act, may be varied by the consent of all the partners, and such consent may be either express or inferred from a course of dealing."

This means that although a partnership agreement may set out the initial intention for heritable property to be excluded from the business, it may be brought into account by the actions of the partners.

That is why additional evidence should be reviewed.

<u>Title deeds</u>

The title deeds may state title is held by an individual or individuals, or it may say title is held in the name of a firm, or by parties as partners of a partnership.

If the title appears to be held by the partnership in this manner, this may suggest it forms part of the business.

In *Jack* v *Jack*[143], the deeds were used as additional evidence. Lord Drummond Young explained:

> "*Lord Hardie [in Marshall v Marshall, 2007 Fam LR 48] held that, in determining whether the farms were partnership property … it was*

---

143 *Jack* v *Jack* [2016] CSIH 75.

> *necessary to go beyond the terms of the recorded heritable title and consider further evidence ... We agree entirely with that approach, which we have attempted to follow in this opinion. We are nevertheless of opinion that the terms of the heritable title are, in the circumstances of the present case, of some importance. The terms of the disposition of 1997 and the corrective disposition of 2001 in favour of the pursuer for love, favour and affection form an important element in the evidence as to whether Torbanehill Mains Farm was considered by the pursuer's father to be partnership property...*"[144]

In this case, a father was a sole trader with two farms. He gifted one to his wife, and one to his son, and the wife and son entered a new partnership using those farms. In this case, they looked at the dispositions as additional (but not the only) evidence. It was felt that the consideration of love, favour and affection, and the fact no SDLT (as it was then) was paid on the transfer, were strong indicators the transfers were to individuals and not a partnership.

<u>Accounts and business balance sheet</u>

Likewise, the partnership accounts can be reviewed to ascertain if the heritable property is shown on the balance sheet as forming part of the business' assets.

In *Jack* v *Jack*, Lord Drummond Young expressed:

> "*If it had been intended that the land should be partnership property, it should have been included as an asset, and the fact that it was not is in our opinion a strong indication that there was no intention on the part of any of the persons involved... that the land should be partnership property...*"[145]

---

[144] Ib id at 183.

[145] Ib id at 182.

Although inclusion on the balance sheet may be a "strong indication", it will still depend on the facts and circumstances.

Ham v *Bell*[146] gives a good account of what type of evidence will be considered. In this case, there was a partnership between a husband and wife which ceased, and a new partnership was formed with their son. The accountants prepared accounts that included the farm on the balance sheet from when the new partnership started in 1998 until 2003. When new accountants were instructed this was corrected and all accounts after that time did not include the farm on the balance sheet. The son had tried to rely on the earlier accounts that the farm was indeed part of the partnership, but the court held that the inclusion within the accounts in the earlier years was a mistake.

Judge McCahill QC commented:

> "*... by mistake they continued to show the farm as an asset of the new partnership. It was a mistake, because I am satisfied that there was no agreement between John and his parents, express or implied, that the farm would become an asset of the new partnership. That mistake was corrected in the 2004 accounts and the correction was then duplicated in the accounts for the ensuing years...*"[147]

The main point from this case is that accounts are not the decisive factor in whether an asset is partnership property or not, they will still need to be considered in light of the circumstances. Judge McCahill QC further commented:

> "*Accounts, therefore, are no more than evidence and if they do not reflect what was agreed they fall to be disregarded.*"[148]

---

[146] *Ham* v *Bell* [2016] EWHC 1791.

[147] Ib id at para 67.

[148] Ib id at para 52.

Ham v *Bell*[149] is an English case and, as such, is not binding in Scotland. However, it is useful authority of what a court may look at in determining whether the accounts accurately reflect the intentions of the parties.

Source of funds for purchase

As the legislation[150] deems property to be partnership property if it was bought with funds from the firm (subject to any contrary intention), the source of the purchase may need to be considered.

In the family law case, *Marshall* v *Marshall*[151], Lord Hardie commented:

> "*s21 assumes that property purchased with money belonging to the partnership was bought on account of the firm unless the contrary intention appears. Thus where an individual partner uses partnership money to purchase heritable property and the title to that is taken in his name alone, ... [these] situations will involve the court in enquiring into the nature of a transaction involving heritable property despite the terms of the feudal title*"[152]

In this case, two brothers held title to a property, which was excluded from the balance sheet, but it had been purchased from partnership funds and there didn't appear to be a contrary intention other than for it to be partnership property. The fact that it was not shown on the balance sheet was held to be irrelevant and down to a different accounting practice.

Tax reporting / documents

If there have been any partial sales of land, which have been split off from a larger title, and these were reported on the partnership tax return and

---

149 Ib id.

150 s21 Partnership Act 1890.

151 *Marshall* v *Marshall* 2007 Fam LR 48.

152 Ib id, at 50.

provided to the partners for their own tax reporting, then this may also suggest the asset was part of a business.

In *Jack* v *Jack*[153], it was suggested that if there was a transfer to a partnership, SDLT would have been payable. Land and Buildings Transaction Tax is now payable where there is a transfer of a chargeable interest to a partnership, under Part 4 of schedule 17 to the Land & Building Transaction Tax (Scotland) Act 2013. As such, checking to see whether LBTT was paid on such a transfer may provide evidence.

---

153 *Jack* v *Jack* [2016] CSIH 75.

CHAPTER TEN

VALUING THE MOVEABLE ESTATE

Basic Principles

As legal rights are based on "*the moveable estate left by the deceased*"[154], the starting point is to use the value of the assets at date of death.

Moss' Trustees v *Moss*[155] confirmed:

> "*The trustees cannot be compelled by the widow to realise the whole moveable estate; but, if they decide not to do so, I think that they must submit to a valuation being made, and that as at the date of death.*"[156]

As there is no requirement to realise the estate, it is also then accepted that an estimated value as at the date of death can be used. In *Gilchrist* v *Gilchrist's Trustees*[157] Lord Adam noted:

> "*[T]he Trustees may resolve not to realise the whole or any part of the Estate and in that case the value must be estimated at the Truster's death.*"[158]

If estate is realised, there are two possibilities that can arise:-

1) There may be a profit or loss incurred when the asset is sold; or

---

154 *Selsdon* v *Selsdon* 1934 SC (HL) 24, per Lord Thankerton at 31.

155 *Moss' Trustees* v *Moss* 1916 1 SLT 321.

156 Ib id, per Lord Hunter at 323.

157 *Gilchrist* v *Gilchrist's Trustees* (1889) 16 R 1118.

158 Ib id, at 1123.

2) The sale value may be higher or lower than the estimate and this may not reflect profit or loss, but merely the fact that an over or under-estimate was used initially.

This chapter will discuss each, below.

Profits / losses on realisation

The authority, discussed below, supports the position that actual profit or loss does not impact on the legal rights calculation. In *Moss' Trustees* v *Moss*[159] the court explained that:

> "*A widow is entitled on her husband's death to one-third of the free moveable estate left by him; for that amount she is creditor on the estate. She is not a beneficiary and is therefore not affected by appreciation or depreciation in the value of the estate administered by the trustees for the beneficiaries. If the trustees proceed at once or within a reasonable time after death to the realisation of the estate, the price so obtained may be conclusive of or it may be taken as an element in determining the value of the estate at death.*"[160]

Likewise, in *Earl of Dalhousie* v *Crokat*[161] Lord Ardmillan commented that:

> "*Legitim must be calculated as at the date of the father's death and profit or loss arising after realisation, in consequence of the Executors mode of dealing with the funds, cannot augment or diminish the claim of the child.*"[162]

---

159 *Moss' Trustees* v *Moss* op cit.

160 Ib id, at 323.

161 *Earl of Dalhousie* v *Crokat* 1868 6 M 659.

162 Ib id at 669.

In *Russel* v *Attorney General*[163] the court held:

> "*... no subsequent change in value, either of decrease or increase, which occurred in the course of the subsequent management of the estate by the executor will diminish or enlarge the value of the jus relicti. It follows that the amount of the petitioner's claim is not affected by reason of the depreciation in value of the investments referred to in the question.*"[164]

Whilst the authority cited above specifically relates to where there has been profit or loss, and confirmed it ought to be excluded, there is authority, discussed below, that suggests realised values ought to be used (albeit it is unclear whether this may relate to scenarios where the realised value is to be taken as the date of death of value, rather than where there has been an actual profit or loss).

In *Gilchrist* v *Gilchrist's Trustees*[165] Lord Adam noted:

> "*The trustees are entitled to realise the estate or any part of it, and had they done so, the amount so realised under the deduction of expenses of the realisation would be the value of the Estate of which the Pursuer is entitled to a share.*"[166]

Lord Shand went on to state:

> "*What a son claiming legitim is entitled to is a share of the value of the Estate, that is, share of the amount which the Estate would bring if it were realised ... In short, if the Estate is to be realised as for all*

---

163 *Russel* v *Attorney General* 1917 SC 28.

164 Ib id at 34.

165 *Gilchrist* v *Gilchrist's Trustees* (1889) 16 R 1118.

166 Ib id at 1122 – 1123.

> *concerned, then the actual realisation in the ordinary course carried out with due diligence and prudence is the amount to be looked to.*"[167]

This case, however, was concerned with shares in ships that were sold within 6 months, and the dicta suggests that the realised value is to be used rather than speculating over another value[168]. Whilst there is discussion about the pursuer being entitled to profit, the decision appears to have been made on the basis that the realised value ought to reflect the date of death value.

Looking at case law since both *Russell*[169] and *Gilchrist*[170], there is authority for substituting realised values where these have been lower than the date of death value, but this is author is not aware of any judicial authority where the contrary has occurred, and a profit has had the effect of enlarging an entitlement to legal rights.

In *Warrack* v *Warracks Trustees*[171], shares had depreciated in value between 1930, the date of death, and 1932 when they were realised.

In this case, Lord Pitman did recognise that there were exceptional circumstances (the economic depression) that impacted on the value and noted in particular:

> "*Seldom, if ever, has a body of trustees had such problems to face. In many markets business on the Stock Exchange had nearly come to a standstill. Acute depression overshadowed all markets, and the trustees had great difficulty.*"

---

167 Ib id at 1124.

168 Lord Shand commented *"there is no need for speculation, as the actual value is ascertained by the sale"*, ib id at 1126.

169 Op cit.

170 Op cit.

171 *Warrack* v *Warracks Trustees* 1934 SLT 302.

The court held that there had not been undue delay in realising the shares and allowed the lower realised value to be substituted, i.e. for the losses to be deducted in ascertaining the value of legal rights.

As such, whilst the earlier authority seems to suggest that losses won't impact on the legal rights calculation, this is authority that a court may take an alternate view depending on the circumstances. This may be useful for trustees who administered estates during the 2020-21 coronavirus pandemic when the markets fell dramatically in the initial period.

Substitution of realised value for estimate

The second scenario is where an estimated value was used as the date of death value, but the asset is later realised for a higher or lower sum. In this case, arguments can be led that the estimated value was an under or over-estimate and ought to be replaced.

The *Gilchrist* case is authority for substituting realised values for estimates, and the other authority, discussed below, is generally supportive of this position.

This can be seen in *Milne* v *Milne's Trustees*[172] where an estimated value at date of death was placed on the business, but that business was subsequently realised and sold, and the court allowed the sale price to be substituted for the date of death value.

Reference was made to earlier cases whereby an estimated value at date of death was to be used where necessary, but in this case because there had been a realisation Lord Moncrieff's view was that the value:

---

172 *Milne* v *Milne's Trustees* 1931 SLT 336.

> "*...must be measured by the amount actually "realised" by the trustees and not by a mere estimate of values*"[173]

Lord Guthrie expressed a similar view in *Alexander* v *Alexander's Trustees*[174]:

> "*...where there has been realisation in ordinary course, the actual realised value and not the estimated value as at the date of death of the deceased determines the quantum of the moveable estate for the purpose of determining the value of legal rights.*"[175]

This case analysed several of the cases mentioned already including *Russel* and *Gilchrist*, and allowed the realised values (being substantially less than estimated value at death) to be substituted.

It is unclear to what extent the courts draw a distinction between what is profit or loss incurred in the administration of the estate, and what is an estimated value that requires to be substituted. As with many areas of legal rights, this can lead to uncertainty and often the position requires to be agreed between the legal rights claimants, the executors and the residuary beneficiaries as to the method of valuation.

---

173 Ib id, at 337.

174 *Alexander* v *Alexander's Trustees* 1954 SC 436.

175 Ib id at 440.

CHAPTER ELEVEN

ISSUES WITH VALUING THE MOVEABLE ESTATE

General principles

As we've just discussed the general position for valuation is that the value to be considered is the value at date of death. This will be straightforward for assets such as bank accounts or refunds due to an estate where there is a specific cash value.

As also expressed, where an asset will not be realised, it may be necessary to place an estimated value on it. This will generally be the same valuation process as is used for tax purposes, in other words what you would expect to receive for the asset if you were to sell it on the open market in its current condition.

However, issues might may still arise when it comes to the valuation certain assets, for example:

- Bank accounts held jointly and ascertaining the share to include
- Valuing an interest in a partnership
- Valuing an interest in a private company

This list is not exhaustive, but is designed to highlight some of the key areas of contention that often crop up, which are discussed further below.

Joint bank accounts

There is, again, sometimes a general presumption that ownership is held 50/50, and that a 50% share of any jointly held bank account ought to form part of the moveable estate. This, however, can misrepresent the true position and inflate or undervalue a legal rights claim where the contributions made were, in fact, different.

There is case law that suggests the correct method is to consider who contributed the funds to the account, and that the exception to this rule would be where an account was used jointly as a household account.

In *Forrest-Hamilton's Trustee* v *Forrest-Hamilton*[176], despite the fact that there were six accounts that the deceased had held in joint names with his spouse, it was held by the court that five were to be treated as his funds alone and only one as a joint account. This was on the basis that he had deposited the sums into all of the accounts. The one account that was deemed to be jointly owned was used for joint household expenses during the course of the marriage.

That said, the joint account in this case was held to be regulated by s1 of the Married Women's Property Act 1964, which has since been repealed[177], so it is unclear whether the same approach would still be taken.

As such, where joint bank accounts are listed, practitioners ought to consider who contributed the funds and for what purpose the account was used to ascertain whether the funds ought to be included in full, in part, or excluded from a legal rights calculation.

Valuing partnerships

For legal rights purposes, what is included in the net moveable estate is the estate "left by the deceased"[178].

---

176 *Forrest-Hamilton's Trustee* v *Forrest-Hamilton* 1970 SLT 338.

177 Repealed by ss28(2) and 29(4) Family Law (Scotland) Act 1985.

178 *Selsdon* v *Selsdon* 1934 SC (HL) 24, per Lord Thankerton at 31.

Therefore, practitioners should consider what is actually left by the deceased in terms of a partnership and this may involve reviewing the terms of a partnership agreement to ascertain what is to happen on death.

In *Ventisei* v *Ventisei's Executors*[179], the partnership agreement contained a clause as follows:

> "*In the event of... death ... the share of the deceased ... partner as brought out in the balance sheet prepared by the accountant of the partnership without taking into account any value for goodwill as at the date of such death ...shall be paid to his or her executor.*"[180]

In this case, no value was placed on goodwill when calculating the deceased partner's share of the partnership. It was argued that goodwill ought to have been included in valuing the partnership for legal rights purposes.

The court held that because all the executors were entitled to was the sum from the partnership calculated in the manner set out in the agreement, goodwill was to be excluded in calculating legal rights.

The Lord President (Clyde) considered the position as to whether the goodwill was "left" by the deceased at the time of death, but concluded that it was merely a contingent interest, so it was not left to the estate. Some useful dicta from the case is:

> "*...Mr Ventisei did not have anything more than a contingent right, dependent on his survival, to the goodwill. At the moment of his death that contingent right flew off and there was, therefore, nothing in respect of goodwill which then belonged to him or to his estate. ... The goodwill of this partnership business was in no sense whatever left by the husband. On the contrary his death finally foreclosed any possibility that he could ever leave it, and on his death nothing in respect of goodwill passed to his estate. For in 1957 when he signed the contract*

---

179 *Ventisei* v *Ventisei's Executors* 1966 SC 21.

180 Ib id at 22.

> *of co-partnery he had agreed that if the other partner survived him the business and goodwill would pass to her.*"[181]

A partnership agreement may also stipulate how gains or losses on realisation are to be included if the partnership is dissolved on a death. This can be seen in the case of *Miller* v *Pollock*[182], in which the partnership agreement read:

> "*...the representatives of the deceased partner are entitled to be repaid the sum at credit of his or her current and Capital accounts ... In ascertaining the sum at credit of a partner's account any appreciation or depreciation arising as a result of revaluation or sale of partnership assets shall be allocated among the partners in proportion to the sums at credit of their respective Capital Accounts as shown in the balance sheet immediately preceding such revaluation or sale...*"[183]

This case is also a useful example of issues that can occur where the partners are unable to agree the accounts. In this case, the court recognised that it is not possible for a legal rights sum to be ascertained until the partnership accounts are finalised and signed.

As part of the case, it was alleged that the solicitor executor had somehow not acted reasonably by not finalising the legal rights calculation earlier. However, in the judgment Lord Burns noted as follows:

> "*...the executor was not entitled to those assets but only to a capital sum represented by the sum at credit in the dissolution accounts. That sum was only ascertained when the accounts were agreed. Mr Reith's position as solicitor to the executory was that he could not arrive at any accurate figure for the value of legal rights until the brothers had agreed*

---

181 Ib id at 25.

182 *Miller* v *Pollock* [2016] CSOH 30.

183 Ib id at para 54.

> *the dissolution accounts and thus could make no final payment until those accounts had been signed off. I consider he was correct in that.*"[184]

Valuing private companies

When it comes to valuing private companies, there are special valuation practices for minority shareholdings.

A minority shareholding is where, for example, a person holds 5% of the shares. Simply placing a pro rata value on the shares as 5% of the business would not reflect the fact the 5% holding is in the minority and does not have much power as, say, a 75% holding.

As such, there is often a reduction placed on minority holdings to reflect this position.

Blackburne J in *Irvine* v *Irvine*[185], noted:

> "*A minority shareholding . . . is to be valued for what it is, a minority shareholding, unless there is some good reason to attribute to it a pro rata share of the overall value of the company. Short of a quasi-partnership or some other exceptional circumstances, there is no reason to accord to it a quality which it lacks.*" [186]

So, if you are acting for executors, care should be taken when instructing valuations as to whether a reduction is appropriate where the deceased had a minority holding.

---

[184] Ib id at para 59.

[185] *Irvine* v *Irvine* (no 2) [2007] 1 BCLC 445.

[186] Ib id, at para 11.

CHAPTER TWELVE

DEDUCTIONS FROM GROSS MOVEABLE ESTATE

General principles

Having established the gross moveable estate, deductions can then be made to ascertain the net moveable estate from which legal rights are payable.

The leading case on what deductions can be made is *Russel v Attorney General*[187].

In this case, there were specific questions raised as to whether certain costs could be offset. In answering the questions, the Court of Session noted in their Order:

> "*We know of no costs and charges other than those mentioned in paragraph 20 of the case which ought to be deducted in ascertaining the amount of the jus relicti.*"[188]

This seems to be authority for the fact that the expenses listed under paragraph 20 of that case are therefore deductible. These are:-

1) *"the [deceased's] separate debts;*

2) *[the deceased's] funeral expenses;*

3) *the expenses of obtaining probate of [the deceased's] will and the estate duty on her moveable property;*

---

[187] *Russel v Attorney General* 1917 SC 28.

[188] Ib id at 34.

4) *[Specific to case]*

5) *the costs properly incurred by the executor in ingathering and inventorying the estate;*

6) *the costs properly incurred by the executor in making and adjusting with the Inland Revenue authorities the valuations for the purpose of the estate duty;*

7) *the costs properly incurred by the executor in ascertaining the testatrix's debts and procuring their discharge; and*

8) *the costs properly incurred by the executor in connection with the realisation in the ordinary course of the testatrix's assets"*[189]

Debts of the deceased

It is generally accepted that any debts that would be deductible for the purposes of inheritance tax would, likewise, be deductible for legal rights purposes.

For "debts", these are any sums the deceased owed at the time of their death and which sums are properly due and will reduce the estate that is "left" to form part of the estate to be distributed for the purposes of legitim and on ward distribution.

The only exclusion for legal rights purposes is that debts that are heritable in nature, i.e. because they are secured on heritable property, are not deductible as they do not reduce the value of the moveable estate, except and unless the value of the debt exceeds the value of the heritable property and a portion of the debt falls to be met from the moveable estate.

[189] Ib id at 32.

Funeral expenses

For "funeral expenses", this will generally be any costs incurred in relation to the funeral, including any memorial service, later interment, headstone engraving, funeral tea and so on.

For inheritance tax purposes, HMRC's guidance is that expenses are deductible unless they are "wholly unreasonable or large in relation to the estate as a whole"[190].

If there was a funeral plan taken out, then it is only the costs that are not covered by that plan that are deductible. This is because the funeral costs won't reduce the moveable estate "left" by the deceased since the moveable estate was reduced in lifetime prior to death and to deduct the costs again would be double-counting.

If a funeral plan covers costs of £3,900 for the funeral, but there are expenses paid for a funeral tea of £500, the £500 would be deductible, but the £3,900 would be ignored for the purposes of calculating legal rights.

Inheritance tax ("IHT") on moveables

The IHT payable on the moveable estate can also be deducted in calculating legal rights.

Because the IHT reduces the moveable estate "left" by the deceased, it follows that the IHT would be deductible.

When calculating IHT on an estate, it will be divided into IHT due on the heritable estate and IHT due on moveables, it is therefore only the IHT on the moveables due to be deducted.

In some scenarios, IHT will may be apportioned across heritable estate, moveable estate, failed potentially exempt transfers, gifts with

---

190 IHTM10371.

reservation, survivorship property, and / or trusts. In such cases, it remains that it would just be the IHT specifically apportioned to the moveable estate that is deductible, since the burden of tax on the other matters will not reduce the moveable estate of the deceased.

As the IHT position is not finalised until clearance has been obtained from HMRC, it is possible that the IHT position will vary as the estate progresses and that the allocation of IHT between moveable and heritable may, likewise, increase or decrease. Depending on the stage of the estate administration when legal rights are calculated and agreed, practitioners may want to bear this in mind (see below re: costs negotiating tax with HMRC).

It is unclear as to whether interest on IHT is deductible. On the one hand, it does not deplete the moveable estate left by the deceased and it is within the executors' control whether interest will or will not apply. However, there may be situations where moveable estate cannot be realised in order to pay the necessary IHT when it falls due on the moveable estate, perhaps because it is a partnership or interest in a company, in which arguably that interest is a cost "properly incurred" in ingathering the moveable estate, which would fall within the later categories listed under paragraph 20.

Costs agreeing the debts

Point 7 from paragraph 20 in *Russel*[191] confirms costs properly incurred in ascertaining and discharging the debts can be deducted. This may be valuation costs, costs liaising with creditors to ascertain the extent of the debt and so on.

As legal rights themselves are a debt on the estate, then arguably the legal costs of ascertaining and agreeing the value of legal rights with parties are also deductible. This may be preparing the legal rights calculation,

---

[191] Op cit.

agreeing it, corresponding with potential claimants, and amending the calculation (this is not an exhaustive list).

In *Russel*[192], there was a query whether the costs of a conditional agreement to deal with legal rights and the court action that followed could be deducted. These were costs incurred by the legal rights claimant and not the estate; they were therefore not allowed to be deducted from the moveable estate for the purpose of calculating legal rights, on the basis they were not incurred in the executry administration.

Some practitioners have suggested that, by extension, this would imply the costs of disputing matters regarding legal rights are not deductible, for example the costs of disputing quantifications. That appears to be reading more into what was said in the case than is written.

How this is applied in practice will vary from practice to practice.

Other estate costs

It is interesting how broad points (5), (6) and (8) of paragraph 20 appear to be.

Firstly, there is no distinction made in the wording of these points between the heritable and moveable property, whereas in (3) there was a distinction made[193].

It therefore appears that all costs incurred in ingathering and inventorying the estate would be deductible, as well as all costs liaising with HMRC regardless of whether the assets are moveable. Arguably, only the costs relating to the moveable estate should be deductible, but

---

192 Ib id.

193 i.e. it specified that it is only the IHT due on the moveable estate deductible, rather than the IHT as a whole.

that was not made clear in the case, so there is an argument to the contrary.

Finally, point (8), seems, on the face of it, to be a catch-all, as it states any "*costs properly incurred by the executor in connection with the realisation in the ordinary course of the testatrix's assets*"[194] may be deducted.

On one reading, this would mean any legal costs, not just those up to Confirmation, but beyond and into the normal costs of realising those assets, would be deductible.

Until there is further judicial authority to clarify the position, it is for practitioners to deduct costs and agree the position with the legal rights claimants.

Depending on who practitioners act for, whether it is executor or claimant, there is scope to take either position. Often, in practice, it will be a matter for agreement between the parties.

---

[194] Op cit.

CHAPTER THIRTEEN

HOW ARE LEGAL RIGHTS DEALT WITH?

General principles

If a deceased died intestate, legal rights will apply if the estate is not exhausted by a spouse or civil partner's prior rights. In such cases, legal rights vest on death and those entitled to legal rights are not required to decide whether to accept that entitlement or not (they are, however, free to renounce or vary such an entitlement[195]).

If the deceased died testate, then those entitled to legal rights must opt whether to take any entitlement under the Will or not. Such decisions by beneficiaries must be informed decisions to be legally effective, can be seen from the authority discussed in this chapter.

If a person has no entitlement under a Will, then their decision, in some respects, will be easier as the options will be to:

- Accept their entitlement to legal rights, or
- Discharge their entitlement.

If a person does have an entitlement under a Will, then they will need to make an election between the Will (sometimes referred to as their conventional provision) and their legal rights.

---

[195] Parties may wish to renounce their legal rights to avoid the application of collation.

Accepting legal rights

There is no prescribed format that an acceptance of legal rights ought to take, and it may be express or implied.

It is common practice that a receipt is signed acknowledging payment of the sum in respect of their legal rights, and Stair suggests that a receipt is enough.[196]

Best practice would be to obtain something in writing that the claimant is agreeing the sum due to them rather than merely acknowledging receipt. This can avoid queries raised at a later date or claims that they ought to have received more where the amount was not expressly agreed.

Although there is no prescribed format, the Law Society of Scotland does have a style within its Guidance, which can be used.[197] The style not only agrees the sum due, but also states that the claimant has accepted the calculation provided to them by the executors.

Interest on legal rights if accepted

It is well settled law that interest is payable on legal rights from the date of death until the date of payment[198].

---

196 *The Laws of Scotland: Stair Memorial Encyclopaedia,* Vol 25, para 777.

197 See https://www.lawscot.org.uk/members/rules-and-guidance/rules-and-guidance/section-e/division-d/guidance/executry-and-trust-accounting/.

198 *Minto* v Kirkpatrick (1833) 11 S 623.

There is no fixed rate of interest that applies to legal rights[199], it will either be set at the discretion of the court[200] or will be agreed between the parties.

Historically, the courts used a general rate of interest of 5%[201], but would apply different rates in certain circumstances. For example, in *Grant* v *Grant's Trustees*[202], the legitim fund had been invested and earned only around 3.5% on the sum. Whilst the Sheriff-Substitute held that the pursuer was entitled to interest at 5%, but this was reserved on appeal and it was held that interest was restricted to the sums that the trustees actually earned.

The Lord President Cooper in *Kearon* v *Thomson's Trustees*[203] gave a scathing account as to why the courts continued to use a historic general rate of 5% and commented:

> "*It follows that the only justification that can to-day be alleged for the supposed "general rule" of 5 per cent is the dying echo of the last relic of the laws against usury, prolonged, long after it should have been silenced, by that blind adherence to old tradition which is one of the less admirable characteristics of certain aspects of the common law.*"[204]

In displacing the 5% general rate, he went on to comment that the proper approach should be:

---

199 s9(1) Succession (Scotland) Act 1964 applies a rate of 7% of interest to the monetary provision of prior rights, but this does not apply to or extend to legal rights.

200 See Professor M C Meston: Succession (Scotland) Act 1964 W.Green; 5th edition.

201 *Bishop's Trustees* v *Bishop* (1894) 21 R 728.

202 *Grant* v *Grant's Trustees* (1898) 25 R 948.

203 *Kearon* v *Thomson's Trustees* 1949 SC 287.

204 Ib id at 294.

> *"...at least as a first approximation—the rate earned by the estate, ex hypothesi under prudent administration. The matter is so laid down in M'Laren on Wills, p. 585. I suggest that there is an additional check which may properly be borne in mind (especially in a case dealing with a legitim creditor who at least in theory may be slightly differentiated from a legatee), viz., the rate at which the recipient might prudently have invested the money had it been available to him for that purpose at the date of death."*[205]

This approach is suggested by various authors[206] and the proper method of calculating interest is therefore to consider:-

- the actual income (or yield) earned by the estate as against capital;
- the prevailing rates of interest at the time a claim is made; and
- whether these has been any unreasonable delay or mismanagement of the estate assets impacting on the interest earned.

Discharging after a death

If someone with an entitlement to legal rights opts not to take such entitlement they are said to discharge their legal rights.

As with an acceptance, there is no prescribed format, but there is a style available from the Law Society of Scotland[207].

---

[205] Ib id at 295.

[206] See: Gloag and Henderson: The Law of Scotland 14th Ed at 38.11, McDonald: Succession at 4.53.

[207] See https://www.lawscot.org.uk/members/rules-and-guidance/rules-and-guidance/section-e/division-d/guidance/executry-and-trust-accounting/

Discharges made after a death will not increase the entitlement of other parties entitled to legal rights[208]. The discharged amount will revert to the estate to be distributed under the terms of the Will or intestacy, as appropriate.

There are some key principles to be mindful of with discharges, which are:

- A discharge should be absolute;
- Any decision to discharge should be an informed decision and;
- Agents and executors for an estate should advise claimants to seek separate legal advice

<u>Discharge should be absolute</u>

Where a discharge is not absolute, there is scope for a potential claimant to seek legal rights at a later date.

In *Petrie's Trustees v Mander's Trustees*[209], the deceased left a widow a liferent of the estate, with the capital passing to their issue. A child did survive the testator, but later died. The widow had signed a document accepting her entitlement under the Will and discharging her claim to legal rights, but it contained a reservation of which stated she reserved:

> "*...any claim which may become competent to me or my personal representatives to any additional benefit if it should happen that any part of the estate falls to be treated as intestate succession.*"[210]

---

[208] See *Fisher* v *Dixon* (1840) 2 D 1121, *Campbell's Trustees* v *Campbell* (1862) 24 D 1321.

[209] *Petrie's Trustees v Mander's Trustees* 1954 SC 430.

[210] Ib id at 430.

On the widow's death a couple of years later, her executors claimed her legal rights from the estate and the Court held they were entitled to claim her jus relictae on the basis that:

> "*The discharge of legal rights was not absolute and complete, but qualified and restricted by a reservation in favour of the widow's representatives.*"[211]

In practice, the executors have the duty to ensure legal rights are discharged and so if a discharge is received that is not absolute, practitioners should consider whether it is appropriate to seek an absolute discharge, otherwise, it will be necessary to consider how to protect against a future claim.

Decision should be informed

A discharge also ought to be an informed decision. To be fully informed, arguably, the person has to be given a calculation or estimate of their potential legal rights entitlement and, if electing to take a legacy under a Will, they must understand the terms of the Will to which they have elected to take a benefit.

In *Walker* v *Orr's Trustees*[212], the children of a deceased took their conventional entitlement under a Will. On their mother's death, 13 years later, they sought to revoke that election and claim their legal rights entitlement. The revocation was allowed given that they did not have sufficient information to make an informed decision. Lord Strachan commented:

> "*... (1) that the pursuers were not shown a copy of their father's settlement and (2) that they were not told the amount of the estate which he had left. ... they clearly did not and could not know the value of their legal rights. In regard to their conventional provisions, the first paragraph of Mr Black's letter gave them a general statement as to the*

[211] Ib id.

[212] *Walker* v *Orr's Trustees* 1958 SLT 220.

effect of the settlement but ... it would be difficult for them without much fuller explanations to appreciate what exactly their conventional provisions were. ... In the proved absence of knowledge of these material facts I am of opinion that the pursuers' claims for legitim are not now barred either by the letters which they wrote or by the subsequent receipt by them of their conventional provisions."[213]

This therefore resulted in the beneficiaries being required to account for their conventional provisions, but the legal rights claims were then allowed.

In addition, legal advice should always be strongly recommended when notifying any parties of their legal rights, and parties should be reminded that signing a document will have legal effects for them before any discharge is signed.

The courts have also allowed elections to be revoked and for legal rights to be claimed where parties were not advised to take, or not given an opportunity, to take such advice.

In *Donaldson v Tainsh's Trustees*[214], the deceased's interest in his wholesale business was held in a liferent style structure allowing the trustees to pay funds to the widow as she required it, but if she remarried it, the whole capital was to be divided between the children.

The widow was called to a trustees' meeting where the trustees' legal agents were present, and she signed at that meeting a minute accepting her entitlement under the Will and discharging her legal rights. She later remarried, which ended her entitlement. The court held that she was not barred from later claiming her legal rights as she had not made an informed decision.

---

213 Ib id at 221.

214 *Donaldson v Tainsh's Trustees* [1886] SLR 23 680.

The Trustees in this case were criticised in a number of ways. Firstly, Lord Justice-Clerk noted legal advice should have been suggested and stated:

> *"I think that the trustees should not be content with explaining the purpose of the deceased's settlement to the widow themselves, but should insist that she should have legal assistance."*[215]
>
> "*…the trustees should see that she makes her election, not from feelings arising from some emotional desire to carry out what she may suppose to have been her husband's wishes, but from a calm and rational consideration of the circumstances.*"[216]

Lord Young and Lord Craighill further criticised the trustees for the circumstances that led to the signing of the discharge[217].

Practitioners should therefore take care that discharges are signed where parties have obtained the proper advice to avoid legal rights claims being allowed at a later date.

Discharge before death

It is possible for parties to discharge their legal rights during their lifetime. Whether or not such a discharge is enforceable will depend on the wording and circumstances, discussed further below.

The effect of a lifetime discharge is to treat the legal rights claimant as predeceasing. This means if there are two children, for example, and one

---

[215] Ib id at 681.

[216] Ib id.

[217] Ib id, Lord Young in particular commented "*I look with great suspicion at this meeting of trustees called at such an early date, and with the desire to get her to put her name to a paper containing a resolution so foolish…*" at 682.

signed a lifetime discharge, the second child would be entitled to receive the whole legitim fund.

As this is a legal fiction and the child has not, in reality, predeceased, it means that representation would not apply to allow their children to claim in their place where they have discharged their rights in life[218].

Enforceability of lifetime discharges

Arguably, because it is not a fully informed decision since they cannot possibly know their entitlement under a Will at that time, it may not bar them from claiming on a death.

If legal advice was given, and the decision was made in full understanding of that advice, then it may be more likely to stand.

Any discharges also ought to be express and clear to avoid ambiguity on later interpretation. In the case of *Price* v *Baxter*[219] a minute of agreement (setting out provisions on separation) purported to discharge legal rights, the wording the minute was as follows:

> "*Both parties hereby renounce and discharge for all time coming his or her respective legal rights of jus relicti and jus relictae and also any prior rights and other rights of succession which may arise on the death of the other party under the Succession (Scotland) Act 1964 or any amendment or re-enactment thereof or at Common Law, and they hereby discharge each other's Executors accordingly.*"[220]

The issue with this clause was that it did not state that the parties were renouncing any entitlements they were to receive under a Will, which, if received, could be renounced triggering further entitlements. Sheriff T McCartney commented:

---

[218] *Hog* v *Hog* (1791) Mor 8193; *Panmure* v *Crokat* (1856) 18 D 703.

[219] *Price* v *Baxter* 2009 Fam LR 138.

[220] Ib id at 139.

> *"... [the clause] makes no express reference to rights of succession arising in terms of the will of the other. ... had it been intended that neither party would accept any bequest in terms of the will of the other, this could have been expressly stated."*[221]

With this in mind, practitioners should take care to ensure that any lifetime discharges in such documents do use clear expressions to discharge any entitlements to avoid any ambiguity.

Discharging / accepting by implication

A legal rights claimant can be said to have either accepted or discharged their legal rights by implication, i.e. where there is no express discharge or acceptance in writing, but where they have been deemed to accept or discharge by their actions.

A discharge, for example, may be implied if the beneficiary opts to take their entitlement under the Will and that entitlement was greater;[222] vice versa, an acceptance can be implied if they take payment of a sum shown on a legal rights calculation if they have a lesser or no entitlement in a Will. This is not ideal as it leaves the executors in an uncertain situation and leaves the door open for claims under a Will or under legal rights at a later date.

It is therefore also best practice to obtain an express discharge or election from a legal rights claimant to avoid such issues arising.

There can be scenarios where parties accept their entitlement under the Will, but such elections can be revoked at a later date if they did not have sufficient information and legal advice to make an informed decision.

Where parties have been given all of the information on their entitlement under the Will and they have been given an opportunity to make an

---

221 Ib id at 143.

222 *The Laws of Scotland: Stair Memorial Encyclopaedia,* Vol 25, 775.

election, but omitted to do so, this can be taken to be acquiescence and acceptance of the entitlement under the Will, as can be seen in *Pringle's Executrices* v *Pringle*[223].

If parties did not have the opportunity to make an informed decision (see the earlier noted cases, *Walker*[224] and *Donaldson*[225]), courts may allow revocations of elections.

The fact that a party has not had separate legal advice will not necessarily render an implied acceptance under a Will invalid. In *Harvie's Executors* v *Harvie's Trustees*[226], the widow was bequeathed the farm under her husband's Will and was informed that an election was required. The lady died before a formal election was made and before she received accounts to quantify her potential entitlement. However, the court held an election had been made and Lord Brand commented:

> "*In the instant case there is no suggestion that the deceased's decision to accept the conventional provisions was an election which was injurious to her pecuniary interests, … Nor is there any suggestion that the deceased was motivated by anything other than her own wishes. … I am of opinion that the deceased's lack of independent legal advice was of no consequence and did not prevent her from making a binding election*".[227]

---

[223] *Pringle's Executrices* v *Pringle* (1870) 8 M 622.

[224] Op cit.

[225] Op cit.

[226] *Harvie's Executors* v *Harvie's Trustees* 1981 SLT (Notes) 126.

[227] Ib id at 127.

CHAPTER FOURTEEN

ELECTIONS & FORFEITURE

General principles

As a result of s13 of the 1964 Act, if a person is entitled to receive a benefit both under a Will and by way of legal rights, they will need to elect which to take as they cannot benefit from both their legal rights and their conventional entitlement. s13 states:-

> *"Every testamentary disposition executed after the commencement of this Act by which provision is made in favour of… any issue of the testator and which does not contain a declaration that the provision so made is in full and final satisfaction of the right to any share in the testator's estate to which the spouse*[228] *or the issue, as the case may be, is entitled by virtue of ius relicti, ius relictae or legitim, shall (unless the disposition contains an express provision to the contrary) have effect as if it contained such a declaration."*

This chapter will focus on the position for Wills executed after the commencement of the 1964 Act (i.e. on or after 10 September 1964). For such Wills, the principle of approbate and reprobate is applied, i.e. a person shouldn't inherit both from a Will and from legal rights.

It is important to note that it is the date of execution of the Will that is relevant and not the date of death.

<u>Note re: position pre 1964</u>

Although it may be unlikely that modern estates will have Wills executed prior to 10 September 1964, it is not unheard of.

---

[228] s131(4) of the Civil Partnership Act 2004 replicates this wording for the rights of civil partners.

In the event that a practitioner is dealing with a Will executed before 10 September 1964, it depends on whether the wording of the Will as to whether a claimant could also receive a benefit from the provisions in the Will. This is the principle of "equitable compensation". Due to the unlikelihood of this in practice, this is noted for reference, only.

What does forfeiture look like in practice?

Where a claim to legal rights is made, this produces the legal fiction that the claimant has pre-deceased for the purposes of reading Will[229] and so they are deemed to forfeit their entitlement under the Will.

It depends on what their entitlement under the Will was as to how this is dealt with in practice.

Where the legal rights claimant was entitled to a legacy, they will simply be treated as pre-deceasing and that legacy would fail. If there is a destination-over to their issue, this may also fail (see Forfeiture of all issue, below).

The position is not as straightforward where the claimant was:-

- Entitled to a share of the residue;
- Left a life interest for the duration of their lifetime; or
- Named as a beneficiary of a discretionary trust under the Will.

Forfeiture of a share of residue

If the claimant has a right in the residue, they will also be treated as predeceasing, and their share of the residue will be treated as failing. It will then depend on the wording of the Will as to what happens with

---

[229] *Rose's Trustees* v *Rose* 1916 SC 827.

that share of the residue. If there is an accretion clause, it will be divided out amongst the other residuary beneficiaries as if that party had never survived.

If, however, the Will is silent on what is to happen with a share of residue that fails, it would fall into intestacy and this could create a scenario where the legal rights claimant gets another bite at the cherry[230].

There is, however, authority that a Court may read an intention into the Will that was not there in order to avoid an intestacy[231].

Forfeit of a liferent interest

If the Will leaves an asset or a share of the estate in liferent to a party, and they opt to claim their legal rights, they are treated as predeceasing the deceased and so the liferent does not come into effect[232].

However, it will depend on the terms of the Will as to when vesting in the capital occurs. If the Will states that vesting will occur on any failure of the liferent which covers the scenario where legal are rights are claimed, then vesting can apply and the capital can pass to those named in the Will.

If the Will simply states that the capital will pass on the death of the liferenter, then the legal fiction of their death does not apply.

There is discussion of this in the case of *Munro's Trustees* v *Munro*[233], in which Lord Fraser stated:

> "*It is well settled that an election to take legal rights does not accelerate the date of vesting provided by the settlement (Muirhead v. Muirhead,*

---

230 *Tindall's Trustees* v *Tindall* 1933 SC 419.

231 *Macnaughton* v *Macnaughton's Trustees* 1954 SC 312.

232 See: *Tindall's Trustees* v *Tindall* op cit.

233 *Munro's Trustees* v *Munro* 1971 SC 280.

> *(1890) 17 R (H.L.) 45). In the present case, and in the events, that have happened, the vesting of the whole residue, so far as it is regulated by the trust disposition and settlement, is postponed until the date of death of [the liferenter].*"[234]

If vesting is delayed until the death of the liferenter, then the Trustees may need to retain the income until vesting occurs. This can cause issues with accumulations of income.

Forfeiture & discretionary will trusts

If the legal rights claimant is a potential beneficiary of a discretionary trust created under the Will, then it will depend on the facts and circumstances as to the effect of this.

As it is a discretionary trust, the legal rights claimant has no fixed entitlement in the trust as any entitlement is wholly at the discretion of the trustees, as such if legal rights were claimed, it won't have the same impact as an entitlement to a liferent trust.

In terms of whether or not they ought to still be considered as a beneficiary of the trust, there are differing views amongst practitioners and different approaches have been taken. There appears to be no clear judicial authority on the matter.

On the one hand, some practitioners will take the view that by claiming legal rights, that party is treated as pre-deceasing and therefore there is no requirement for the trustees to consider them as a potential beneficiary of the trust.

However, it may also depend on the circumstances around the trust including any powers of the trustees, or any letter of wishes.

If a testator gives trustees power to add any beneficiary they see fit to the trust deed, without any exclusion to those who claimed legal rights, then,

---

[234] Ib id at 288.

even if a claimant had excluded themselves as a beneficiary, by virtue of the legal fiction of pre-deceasing, the trustees could, using such a power, add them to the class of beneficiaries to be considered.

Likewise, a settlor may want to express wishes in a letter of wishes suggesting that trustees consider a legal rights claimant even if they have claimed legal rights.

Practitioners may come across scenarios where this may be appropriate. For example, if a child has issues with alcohol and drugs, the parent may assume legal rights will be claimed, and take steps to reduce any such entitlement. However, parents often wish to allow for future benefit if their child overcomes such issues, or, alternatively to protect that child should they fall into serious financial difficulty.

A letter of wishes could therefore be prepared expressing that even if that child claimed legal rights, they are still to be considered a beneficiary (perhaps in certain scenarios) and the trustees still ought to provide for him.

On the contrary, there may be an express a wish set out in a letter of wishes that if a child claims legal rights, they are to be excluded from benefiting under the trust under any circumstances, which would also set out the testator's views very clearly for the trustees.

The law is not clear on this at present and courts are often not keen to interfere with trustees' discretion[235] except where:

> "*...it can be shown that the trustees considered the wrong question, or that, although they purported to consider the right question, they did*

---

235 For example, *Orr Ewing* v *Orr Ewing's Trs.* (1884) 11R 600, Lord President Inglis noted "[t]he great principle in the administration of Scotch testamentary trusts is, to leave the administration where the testator himself has placed it, unless from fault or accident the trust has become unworkable..." at 627 – 628.

> *not really apply their minds to it or perversely shut their eyes to the facts or that they did not act honestly or in good faith…"*[236]

With that in mind, provided that trustees properly consider the issue, and act in good faith, when determining whether a legal rights claimant is to benefit, it may be difficult for a court to intervene.

Where practitioners are acting for a legal rights claimant, it ought to be made clear to them the risks in potentially claiming or discharging their legal rights.

When acting for someone at the Will drafting stage, practitioners should also consider whether it would be beneficial to the trustees to put in place a robust letter of wishes.

Forfeiture of all issue

If a legal rights claimant accepts their entitlement to legal rights, they not only forfeit their own entitlement under a Will, but they may also forfeit their children's entitlements depending on the terms of the Will.

Where the word issue is used in s13 of the 1964 Act, this is a reference to issue of all levels, so if the highest level claims, then all descendants of that party forfeit due to the ascendant claiming, unless there is express provision in the Will to the contrary.

This means that if a party claims legal rights, then they may also forfeit any entitlement of their issue. It will very much depend on the terms of the Will and the test set out in *Hurll's Trustees* v *Hurll*[237], as follows:

> "*…the test here is whether the gift to issue is one separate from and independent of that in favour of their [parent]…*"

---

236 *Board of Management for Dundee General Hospital* v *Bell's Trustees* 1952 SC(HL) 78, per Lord Reid at 92.

237 *Hurll's Trustees* v *Hurll* 1964 SC 12.

As such if a descendant's entitlement is linked to and subject to their parent's predeceasing, then it would not be separate from or independent and it would also fail.

> <u>Example</u>
>
> If there is a legacy of £10,000 to A, whom failing the £10,000 is to go equally between A's children, the legacy to A's descendants is not separate from the legacy to A and, as such, s13 would apply. If A were to forfeit that legacy, they would also forfeit that legacy on behalf of their children and the legacy would fail.
>
> If a Will left a legacy of £10,000 to each of the testator's children, and separately, a legacy of £2,500 to each of the testator's grandchildren, these would be separate and distinct entitlements. If a child claimed their legal rights, they would forfeit their own legacy of £10,000, but not the separate legacies of £2,500 to their children.

The same principles apply in the context of the division of the residue. There is therefore a possibility of intestacy applying if all parties' entitlements are forfeit. This could result in the legal rights claimant receiving both their legal rights, and also a share of the residue under intestacy.

In *Tindall's Trustees* v *Tindall*[238], the Will left a liferent in favour of the widow, with a successive liferent for the son. The fee was left to the son's children, i.e. the grandchildren of the deceased. Both the widow and son claimed legal rights. The Court held that by claiming legal rights, the son forfeit not only his own, but his children's entitlements and the whole estate therefore fell into intestacy. The result of which was that the son received the whole intestate estate after the widow's legal rights.

---

238 *Tindall's Trustees* v *Tindall* 1933 SC 419.

Where there is a possibility of intestacy a Court may opt to read an intent into a Will that wasn't expressly stated[239]. Executors cannot read an intention into a Will that is not there, so the default position will be that intestacy applies unless a Court were to deem otherwise. In practice it may be preferable to reach an agreement amongst the potential beneficiaries to avoid the costs of a court action.

---

[239] *Naismith* v *Boyes* (1899) 1 F (HL) 79; *Buyers' Trustees and Nunan* 1981 SC 313

CHAPTER FIFTEEN

COLLATION

What is collation?

Collation, or the Latin maxim "*collatio inter liberos*", applies if two or more claimants to the legitim fund are claiming legal rights and one of them elects for collation to apply.

Collation means that lifetime gifts made to the claimants will be added to the value of the legitim fund in order to calculate what each party is to receive. It is, effectively, a method of equalisation between the parties and the lifetime gifts are treated like an advance of their share of the estate.

The principle is perhaps best expressed in *Monteith* v *Monteith's Trustees*[240], by Lord Rutherford Clark:

> *"Collatio inter liberos has application only when more than one child claims legitim. Its purpose is to require a child who claims legitim to collate the advances which it has received during the lifetime of the father, and thus to make a nominal enlargement of the legitim fund in order to the more equitable distribution of the actual fund."*[241]

Authors have described this as being a means of putting parties who have received advances on equal footing with their siblings[242].

---

240 *Monteith* v *Monteith's Trustees* (1882) 9 R. 982.

241 Ib id at 1,008.

242 See: J McLaren *The Law of Wills and Succession as Administered in Scotland* (3rd edition 1894) at 316.

It does not, however, apply to claims by spouses or civil partners. There is therefore no requirement to collate any gifts made by the deceased to a spouse or civil partner[243].

Key principles

As the intention is to create equality as between the parties, collation is based on the legal fiction that an advance was made from the legitim fund during the deceased's lifetime.

The Lord President expressed the position in *Coats' Trustees*[244] as follows:

> "*It assumes that the father has paid a part or whole of his indebtedness at a time when no relationship of debtor and creditor existed between the father and the child. It further assumes that the payment is made out of the legitim fund although confessedly the legitim fund is at the time non-existent.*"[245]

The Lord President further confirmed that collation only applies to those parties actually claiming legal rights and it does not impact on the position of the other children of the deceased[246].

Representation also applies to collation, so if a child of a pre-deceasing child is claiming legal rights, then any gifts to the pre-deceasing child must be collated[247]. The gifts to be collated are those paid to the pre-deceasing child as well as to the claimant. However, as the amount due to be paid to the claimant may not necessarily be what their parent was

---

243 See *Coats' Trustees* v *Coats* 1914 SC 744.

244 Ib id.

245 Ib id at 748.

246 Ib id,

247 See s11(3) 1964 Act, which confirms those claiming under representation are also required to collate.

entitled to (as it will depend on whether the division is per stirpes or per capita), this may impact on the collation calculation[248].

If collation applies, then the value to be added is the value of the asset at the time the gift is made, not the value of that asset at the testator's death[249].

There is no interest payable on collatable advances, in other words any income the person has received on the sum they received is ignored[250].

The burden is on the executors to prove that an advance was not a gift, but is to be treated as a payment out of the legitim fund, albeit a lower bar than to prove a debt[251].

How is collation calculated?

Collation is calculated by adding the value of the gifts made to the legitim fund, then calculating the sum due to each party (whether per stirpes or per capita). This will then determine how much each party is entitled in total taking into account lifetime advances and their share of the legitim fund.

> <u>Example</u>
>
> The legitim fund is £250,000, to be split between three children, A, B and C, who all claim legal rights. A received a gift of £10,000 and B received a gift of £40,000, which would be added to the legitim fund giving a total collated fund of £300,000.

---

248 See M Meston "*Collation of Advances to Ancestors*" 1967 SLT (News) 224.

249 *Elliots Exx* v *Elliot* 1953 SC 43.

250 *Gilmour's Trs.* v *Gilmour*, 1922 SC 753.

251 See *Welsh* v *Welsh's Trustees* (1878) 5 R 542.

Each would be entitled to 1/3 of £300,000, i.e. £100,000, which is made up of a share of the legitim fund and the advances they have received already. The £250,000 legitim fund would therefore be divided as follows:-

- £100,000 to C (as C never received any gifts)
- £60,000 to B (being £100,000 less the £40,000 received in lifetime)
- £90,000 to A (being £100,000 less the £10,000 received in lifetime)

The calculations may be more complex in practice where representation applies or where there are multiple gifts.

What is a collatable gift?

Three things must be present in order for a gift to be collatable, these are:

- There has been a loss to the testator's moveable estate,
- There was a corresponding increase in the recipient's estate, and
- The intention of the testator was for the gift to be collatable.

There are gifts that will not normally be collatable, because of the nature of the payments, and these will include:-

- Normal payments for the maintenance/education of a child paid by a parent,
- Remuneration for services under a legal contract, since the testator would have received a "benefit" in exchange for the sums paid and would not have had the intention for it to be a gift

- Loans to a child, which can be called up as part of the moveable estate, since there would be no loss to the moveable estate, and
- Gifts of heritable property, which also do not reduce the moveable estate (unless the heritable interest would have been treated as moveable under the principles discussed in earlier chapters).

Where an advance is treated as recompense for services, it has also been held to be non-collatable. This can be seen in *Minto* v *Kirkpatrick* [252]where a son became a partner in the business. Whilst it was a lifetime advance, it was held not to be collatable.

Intention of the testator

In *Monteith* v *Monteith's Trustees*[253], it was accepted that the rules relating to collation are different than those relating to legitim fund, generally, and the eventual purpose is to ensure an equitable distribution of the actual fund and to look at the intention of the donor. Some useful dicta from the case is as follows:

> "*...while it is settled law that the father cannot by testament affect the legitim fund, or remit debts forming part of the moveable succession, it is equally certain that the rules applicable to collation of advances are entirely different, as I have taken occasion to shew. It is admitted that* ***any indication of intention on the part of the father to exclude collation, although of course only designed to operate after his death, will be effectual...***"[254]

> "*...it is clear that he did not intend that his son (the pursuer) should enjoy equal benefit with his daughters, and that it would be*

---

[252] *Minto* v *Kirkpatrick* (1833) 11 S 632.

[253] Op cit.

[254] Ib id Lord Justice Clerk, at 992.

> *unreasonable to impute such intention to him, and act on it as his presumed will. ... **There is no room whatever for presuming an intention** on the father's part that he should have more in order that he might enjoy equal benefit with his sisters. In other words, there is no room for the presumption on which the doctrine of collatio inter liberos rests...*"[255]

Professor Meston has also opined that the intention of the testator is paramount in ascertaining whether collation is to apply[256]. This can result in collation being dis-applied or forced by the testator.

Where the testator had made clear that gifts are intended as outright donations in addition to collation, such gifts would therefore be non-collatable[257].

Authors have suggested that it may be possible for an otherwise non-collatable gift to be brought back into account if a testator stipulates that such payments should be treated as advances[258].

Collation of gifts via other structures

It may also be possible that gifts made indirectly (i.e. where a transfer is made to a partnership or trust, then from that structure to a legal rights claimant) could be brought into account under the principle of collation.

If the key principles are met, i.e. that there is a loss to the testator, a subsequent gain for the recipient and the intention of the testator is for such advances to be considered, then the fact the gifts were not made direct to the recipient won't necessarily preclude them from being

---

255 Ib id, Lord Young, at 995.

256 Opinion 55, Professor M. C. Meston, *Meston's Succession Opinions* W. Green / Sweet & Maxwell 2000.

257 *Grant* v *Gunn's Trs* (1833) 11 S 484.

258 See: Gloag & Henderson 14th Ed at 38.12.

collated[259]. What may need considered is the full facts and circumstances of the transfers and the nexus of payment to the claimant.

[259] See Opinion 55, Professor M. C. Meston, *Meston's Succession Opinions* op cit.

CHAPTER SIXTEEN

INTERACTION WITH INHERITANCE TAX & OTHER TAXES

Inheritance tax

When dealing with legal rights, practitioners should always consider whether there are any IHT implications in a proposed course of action.

IHT will need to be considered in the following scenarios:-

- when a party wishes to discharge their legal rights, as this is a transfer of value
- when a party is entitled to legal rights and is under the age of 18
- when a party is entitled to legal rights and dies before a decision on whether to accept or discharge is made
- when a spouse or civil partner is claiming legal rights and spouse exemption will apply to the assets they receive, particularly if the spouse or civil partner is not domiciled in the UK
- when agricultural or business property relief is being claimed elsewhere in the estate to ensure a tax liability is not triggered inadvertently
- when a claim to legal rights exhausts the residue of the estate and abatement then applies, which may reduce IHT exemptions

Discharge of legal rights

Where a party is entitled to legal rights, if they choose to discharge that entitlement, that is treated as a transfer of value for IHT purposes.

<u>If discharged within 2 years of death</u>

If a discharge is undertaken within 2 years of the date of death of the testator, then the provisions of s142 of the Inheritance Tax Act 1984 (hereafter, the "1984 Act") will apply.

HMRC's IHT Manual[260] at confirms that the meaning of estate for the purposes of 142 does include any entitlement to legal rights under Scots Law.

As such, provided that a discharge is made within 2 years of the date of death, the effect of which is "this Act shall apply as if ... the disclaimed benefit had never been conferred."[261]

As this is a disclaimer of an interest, rather than a variation, there is no requirement for the discharge to specifically elect for s142 to apply[262].

It is also worth remembering that s142 will not apply if there is any consideration given in exchange for the discharge[263]. This means that if a legal rights discharge were signed in exchange for agreeing to receiving a gift from the residuary beneficiary, this may have IHT consequences, per the below.

---

260 At IHTM35071.

261 s142(1) Inheritance Tax Act 1984.

262 s142(2) only applies to variations, "[the provisions] shall not apply to a variation unless the instrument contains a statement, made by all the relevant persons, to the effect that they intend the subsection to apply to the variation".

263 Ib id, s142(3).

If s142 does not apply

If legal rights are not discharged within two years of the date of death, s142(1) will not apply and any discharge after that date will be treated as a potentially exempt transfer for IHT purposes and will be subject to the usual 7-year rule.

This is the also case where s142 does not apply for any other reason, for example if consideration was given in exchange for the discharge.

If legal rights are discharged and are treated as a PET, but the claimant does not survive 7 years, then the value of the legal rights (and any interest until the time when the discharge was made), will need to be brought back into account on the death of the claimant. This may trigger unwanted IHT in the claimant's estate.

If tax is due on the failed PET, this may cause difficulties in practice in identifying the donee liable to tax[264].

Children under 18 entitled to legal rights

Where a child under 18 is entitled to legal rights, s147 of the 1984 Act ought to be considered.

s147 applies if an estate is passing wholly to a surviving spouse or civil partner and is therefore otherwise exempt for IHT, but there are children under 18 entitled to legal rights, which triggers IHT falling due.

The default position, if no action is taken, is set out under s147(2), i.e. executors must settle the tax as if legal rights will be claimed. If legal rights are discharged within 2 years of the child attaining the age of 18, then any tax paid on their respective legal rights can be reclaimed.

s147(3), allows executors to elect to dis-apply s147(2) within 2 years of the date of death, which election must be made in writing. Where this

[264] See s204 re liability of tax, ib id.

election is made, the executors need not pay tax. If legal rights are claimed within 2 years of the child attaining age 18, the proportionate amount of tax requires to be paid.

Interest is applied in the usual manner to any reclaim/payment of tax.

This section, however, only applies where the reason the estate is exempt for IHT purposes is because the whole estate passes to a spouse or civil partner.

There is no provision made in the legislation for a scenario where the whole estate passes to charities and is therefore exempt, but for the application of legal rights. As such, in that scenario, the default position will always apply and there is no option to dis-apply it.

Legal rights claimant dies before decision made

If a person survives a deceased and they vest in their entitlement to legal rights, but they subsequently die before accepting or discharging their legal rights, that entitlement will form part of their estate for IHT purposes.

In this scenario, the value to be included in the estate is both the principal legal rights sum and the interest calculated thereon.

The IHT Manual[265] sets out how legal rights ought to be calculated as an asset in the estate. In this section it confirms that interest can be calculated from the testator's date of death to the claimant's date of death (i.e. provision does not need to be made for future interest).

If the amount of legal rights due has not been ascertained at the time of the testator's death, then an estimate ought to be included and an amended value can be reported to HMRC at a later date once agreed.

---

[265] At IHTM10302.

If the claimant was a child who was under 18, then the provisions of s147 mentioned earlier may apply, in which case the entitlement to legal rights could be discharged within 2 years of death and the sum need not be included as an asset of the estate.

In scenarios where a claimant was entitled to both legal rights and an entitlement under the Will, the executors can make an election. HMRC's Guidance states:

> *"If there was scope for an election and the person entitled has died before exercising it (either expressly or by implication), their executors are entitled (if there is no question of insolvency or abatement of legacies) to exercise the election between legal rights and the testamentary provisions, with the same considerations in mind as would have influenced that person had they been alive. You should refer any case where this applies and the tax at stake is worthwhile to Technical."*[266] –

Spouse or civil partner claiming legal rights

There can be scenarios in practice where a spouse or civil partner finds it more attractive to claim their legal rights than to take their entitlement under a Will, perhaps because the Will does not give them an outright inheritance, but rather an interest in a trust, or perhaps because they are separated and a divorce/dissolution was not finalised before a death.

In such cases, the exemption under s18(1) of the 1984 Act will apply and the full value of any assets or sums received by a spouse or civil partner will be exempt from IHT.

It may therefore not be possible to confirm the actual IHT position for an estate until the legal rights have been agreed and all interest paid to

---

[266] At IHTM12230.

the spouse / civil partner. After which, the IHT on the remainder of the estate passing to non-exempt beneficiaries can be confirmed.

The exemption under s18(1) is also restricted in circumstances where the spouse or civil partner was not also domiciled in Scotland, in which case (for deaths on or after 6 April 2013), any sums they receive by way of legal rights will be exempt up to the value of the nil rate band in place at the time, but any sums or assets received above this amount will trigger IHT and an apportionment of the tax between the spouse / civil partner and other beneficiaries will be necessary.

Agricultural or business property relief claims

There is a quirk in relation to agricultural property relief ("APR") and business property relief ("BPR") and their interaction with other reliefs which comes in the form of s39A of the 1984 Act.

s39A sets out how APR/BPR is allocated in an estate. If there is a specific legacy of assets that qualify for APR/BPR, then the relief attaches to the specific legacy. If, however, there is no specific legacy and the assets that qualify form part of the residue of the estate, then APR/BPR is spread between the residue and other legacies / specific gifts from the estate.

This means that if there is at least one exempt beneficiary to the estate, APR/BPR could be wasted and the actual IHT liability could be higher than practitioners expect.

Because s39A comes into operation where APR/BPR assets fall into the residue, and there are any sums due from the estate to other parties, if legal rights are claimed, this could trigger the application of s39A.

> Example
>
> An estate comprises £3m of which £1.5m is in an investment portfolio (non-qualifying for BPR) and £1.5m is held in a business qualifying for BPR. The whole estate is due to a spouse, but the legitim fund is £1.5m if claimed. If legal

rights are not claimed, s39A does not apply, and the whole estate would be exempt.

If legal rights are claimed, £1.5m will go to the spouse and £1.5m will go to children. However, APR/BPR would not attach to the full £1.5m as there is not a specific legacy to the children. Instead, the £1.5m APR/BPR would be allocated pro-rata.

In this scenario, 50% would be allocated to the spouse and 50% to children. The £1.5m passing to the children via legal rights would only get APR/BPR of £750,000, and this would trigger IHT falling due on the other £750,000 and a tax charge.

This is a very simplistic example, but it shows how a claim to legal rights may trigger an unintentional tax charge if s39A were to apply. In such situations where there are BPR / APR qualifying assets, it may be beneficial for the parties to agree to vary the estate to avoid such an IHT charge.

Practitioners should therefore be mindful of these scenarios and raise other potential methods of varying the estate at the earliest possible stage so that such matters can be considered and evaluated.

Claim for legal rights results in abatement

It is possible that a claim for legal rights could exhaust the residue of an estate and abatement then applies. The order in which legacies are abated is to reduce cash legacies, first, and then specific legacies.

Under IHTA 1984 s37, it is the value of the abated legacy that is to be used for the calculation of IHT, this means that if legal rights triggers abatement, all legacies to exempt beneficiaries need to be recalculated.

This can have the effect of increasing the IHT due by the estate, particularly if the estate had been eligible for the reduced rate of IHT at 36% because of the amount passing to charity. If those legacies are abated and the value passing to charity falls below the 10% required for this reduced rate to apply, then this would trigger the estate being liable at the higher rate of 40%.

Example

An estate consists of £500,000 wholly in cash. There are legacies of £450,000, £50,000 to charities, £400,000 to non-exempt beneficiaries and a residue of £50,000 to other charities. If legal rights are not claimed, £100,000 passes to charities and will be exempt from IHT and will get the reduced rate of IHT on the estate that is liable to IHT over the nil rate band.

If the legitim fund in that example is £250,000 this would exhaust the residue, and the legacies (totalling £450,000) would need abated and to be paid from the remaining £250,000. The charitable legacies are 1/9th of that, i.e. c. £27,000. In that scenario only this amount would be exempt for IHT and the estate would lose the benefit of the reduced rate of IHT.

Careful advice should be given in scenarios where beneficiaries are weighing up options between legacies and legal rights as the tax implications may alter their anticipated inheritance, and it may be appropriate to vary an estate and agree an alternative distribution between beneficiaries to avoid triggering additional IHT.

Income Tax

Legal rights interest is paid to claimants gross, i.e. without the deduction of income tax unless beneficiary is non-resident.

Income tax on legal rights interest is payable in the year or years in which it is actually paid to the claimant[267], regardless of when it was received by the executors.

The executors' liability to income tax is unaffected by payment of interest on legal rights.

In working out the share of income due to the beneficiaries for R185 purposes for those inheriting under the Will, legal rights interest is deducted to work out their notional share[268].

Under s669 of Income Tax (Trading and Other Income) Act 2005 2005 (hereafter, "ITTOIA"), beneficiaries can claim relief on the IHT paid on accrued interest/ex-dividends forming part of their legacy/share of an estate. However, s669 ITTOIA can't be applied to legal rights interest as it is not treated as residuary income within the definition.

Issues may arise for income tax where an election is possible and it is unclear whether a party will take their conventional provision, or their legal rights.

<u>Where an election is possible</u>

In a scenario where a beneficiary is entitled to a specific legacy under a Will, which produces income, the income follows the legacy and is due to be received and reported by that beneficiary.

If that beneficiary is also entitled to legal rights and an election between the legacy and legal rights is required, a question then arises as to what ought to happen with the income.

If the beneficiary opts to take their legal rights, they forfeit the legacy under the Will[269]. That asset and any income on it then forms part of the

---

267 *Sweet* v *Henderson* (1920) 7 TC, 58 SLR 129.

268 s702 Income & Corp taxes act 1988.

269 See earlier chapters on Forfeiture.

residue of the estate, and the liability to settle income tax on it reverts to the executors.

In such situations, prior to a formal election being made, executors should:

- retain the income until an election is made, to ensure they do not distribute it if legal rights are later claimed; and
- provide the beneficiary with a note of all income due on that specific legacy for reporting in their own Income Tax Return.

Where a beneficiary has reported income on a specific legacy that is not later due to them, the tax paid on it can be reclaimed by the beneficiary.

If the reverse occurs and legal rights are claimed, the executors will report the income in the estate and settle the tax due as if that asset had always formed part of the residue.

If relief under s669 ITTOIA was claimed before an election is made and legal rights are later claimed, s669 would be dis-applied and additional tax on previous years may fall due (albeit it may be minimal).

Capital Gains Tax ("CGT")

As has been stated, legal rights claimants have no entitlement to any underlying assets within the estate[270]. As such, they do not vest in any assets and would not be affected by any sales by the executors of assets sold to fund their legal rights.

It may be desirable in some situations for executors to appropriate an asset to legal rights claimants and sell it on their behalf to make use of

---

270 *Cameron's Trustees* v *Maclean* 1917 SC 416.

their annual exemption for CGT purposes, or to utilise lower rates of CGT that the claimant may pay in comparison to the estate.

Practitioners should take care to consider whether the executors have powers to appropriate in this manner prior to doing so. The power must be expressly given within the Will. Often the power to appropriate will read that it may be used to appropriate all or part of an asset in satisfaction of a beneficiary's entitlement under the Will. Where this is the case, as a legal rights claimant is treated as being owed a debt, rather than having an entitlement, care should be taken as to whether the wording of the Will will allow such an appropriation or not.

CHAPTER SEVENTEEN

DEFEATING LEGAL RIGHTS

Can legal rights be defeated?

Practitioners will often be faced with clients who wish to defeat legal rights. Whilst legal rights are an entitlement, there may be methods of minimising the exposure to legal rights. This may be achieved by:-

- converting moveable estate to heritable estate;
- creating moveable debts;
- ensuring life polices and pensions don't form part of the legal rights fund;
- making valid gifts to individuals or trusts from the moveable estate prior to death; or
- forcing intestacy such that prior rights exhaust the estate.

Converting moveable estate to heritable

As has been demonstrated in earlier chapters, legal rights only apply to the net moveable estate. If moveable estate can be converted to heritable estate prior to a death, then this will reduce the value capable of forming part of the legal rights fund without reducing the overall value of the deceased's estate.

Practitioners should carefully consider whether this appropriate for the client if they have ongoing requirements from income that are usually met from the moveable estate, and issues of liquidity if capital will be needed in the future.

Creating moveable debts

To further reduce the moveable estate, parties may wish to consider taking loans on unsecured terms in order to purchase additional heritable property, or to make gifts (see below) from the estate. By increasing the moveable debts, this will reduce the net moveable estate for legal rights purposes.

The difficulty in practice is that where significant sums are involved, lenders would usually seek a security, which would defeat the purpose of the exercise. Loans from friends or family could be made, but there may be IHT implications of doing so[271].

Making valid gifts

As set out in chapter 6, gifts are only brought back into account where a testator has not fully divested themselves of the assets. As such, it is possible to make various lifetime gifts to reduce the estate on death for legal rights purposes.

Chapter 6 sets out the position in further detail, but care should be taken to ensure no benefit is retained where gifts are made to individuals, and that it is clear the intention was for the advance to be gift. To avoid collation applying to the gift, the testator may also wish to make this clear[272].

As explained in chapter 6, gifts can be made to create liferent trusts, which reserve an interest in the income of the gifted assets. However, for gifts to discretionary trusts, care should be taken to ensure:-

- the settlor is not a beneficiary; and

---

[271] See s103 Finance Act 1986.

[272] See chapter 15 for more on collation.

- the trust deed does not allow for reversion to the settlor.

Forcing Intestacy

Finally, practitioners may wish to consider whether the provisions under intestacy may be preferable. As legal rights are only payable after prior rights have been settled, if prior rights would exhaust the estate, it may be an option to force intestacy and for the whole estate to pass to the surviving spouse or civil partner.

Even where a Will exists, if intestacy is triggered to the whole estate, prior rights will take preference to any claim for legal rights. This can be seen in the case of *Kerr, Petitioner*[273], where the whole estate was left to the widow, but a claim for legal rights was raised by her stepdaughter (the deceased's daughter). The widow renounced her interest in the estate forcing intestacy. In this case, the whole estate fell to be administered as intestate estate and the widow's prior rights exhausted the estate, defeating the claim for legal rights.

The Sheriff in the case commented:

> "*The effect of the definition of "intestate" in s. 36 (1) of the 1964 Act is, in my opinion, that there is intestacy when there is no will at all,* ***and also when there is a will which becomes wholly or partly inoperable****. ... In my opinion estate which is not in fact disposed of by testamentary disposition must necessarily be intestate estate, with the result that s. 9 (1) of the Succession (Scotland) Act 1964 applies to it.*"[274]

Some practitioners will often prepare Wills that appoint executors, alone, which are valid testamentary writings for the purposes of avoiding the requirement to seek the appointment of an executor-

---

[273] 1968 SLT (Sh Ct) 61.

[274] Ib id at 63.

dative. However, in the absence of a residue clause, the Will is wholly inoperable and the principles in *Kerr*[275], above, would apply.

[275] Ib id.

CHAPTER EIGHTEEN

THE FUTURE OF LEGAL RIGHTS

Are legal rights here to stay?

There have not been any substantive changes in the law of succession for over fifty years and the 1964 Act remains the key legislation, whilst most of the law on legal rights is still based on common law judgments.

For the time being, it appears that legal rights are here to stay and there are currently no plans to make substantive changes to the law on legal rights, or the law on succession, generally, without further consultation.

That said, there have been various Consultations and Reports over the past 10 to 15 years seeking views on legal rights and potential proposals for reform.

Timeline of recent succession projects

The recent projects have included:-

- in 2009, the Scottish Law Commission published their Report on Succession[276];
- in 2015, the Scottish Government's undertook a Consultation on the law of Succession[277];

---

276 https://www.scotlawcom.gov.uk/files/7112/7989/7451/rep215.pdf

277 Scottish Law Commission: *Consultation on the law of Succession*, https://www.webarchive.org.uk/wayback/archive/20150828184326/http://www.gov.scot/Publications/2015/06/7518/downloads#res480484

- in 2016, the Succession (Scotland) Act 2016 came into force reforming a few ancillary matters;
- in 2018, the Scottish Government's Response to the 2015 Consultation was published[278];
- in 2019, a further Consultation on the law of Succession was launched by the Scottish Government; and
- in 2020, the Scottish Government's Response to the 2019 Consultation was published[279].

Of these, the key consultation that considered legal rights was the 2015 Consultation. Following this, the 2019 Consultation focussed on the division of estates under the laws of intestacy, although it did also consult on the rights of stepchildren and cohabitants to have a potential entitlement to an estate.

What did the 2015 consultation ask?

Chapter 3 of the Consultation[280] focussed on disinheritance from estates where there is a Will in place.

---

278 https://www.webarchive.org.uk/wayback/archive/20181226070023/https://www2.gov.scot/Topics/Justice/law/damages/succession/scottish-government-response-succession-consultati

279 https://www.gov.scot/binaries/content/documents/govscot/publications/consultation-analysis/2020/05/scottish-government-response-consultation-law-succession/documents/scottish-government-response-consultation-law-succession/scottish-government-response-consultation-law-succession/govscot%3Adocument/scottish-government-response-consultation-law-succession.pdf

280 Scottish Law Commission: *Consultation on the law of Succession*, op cit.

It referred to the earlier 2009 Report and the Consultation suggested the current system is flawed because of the ability for people to avoid legal rights by ensuring their estate consists mostly or heritable property.

The Consultation commented:

> "*...the tension therefore lies between striking the appropriate balance between individuals having freedom to leave their property to whoever they want and giving family some rights to receive an inheritance...*"[281]

The reform therefore looked at key topics, including:-

- who should be protected from being disinherited;
- What percentage of the estate should a "legal share" amount to for such persons;
- Whether the distinction between heritable and moveable property should be removed and, if so, should "agricultural units" be excluded;
- Whether to remove the requirement for "collation"; and
- How a "legal share" might be paid in practice, i.e. might there be an option for payment by instalments.

Who should be protected?

Chapter 2 of this Book sets out who, at present, is entitled to claim legal rights and the proposal in the Consultation was for a spouse/civil partner to remain capable of claiming a "legal share" from the estate.

What was consulted on was whether there ought to be any change to whether all "issue" of the deceased ought to be entitled, or whether legal

---

[281] Ib id at 3.6.

rights should be amended to instead provide for "dependent" children, i.e. those under 18 or 25 depending on whether they are in full time education.

What percentage should the legal share be?

The suggested amount for spouses/civils partners was 25% of what they would have received if the deceased died intestate (albeit there were proposed changes to intestacy so it would not equate to the same sums as we have under the current law).

For issue, two options were put forward:-

- Option 1 was to give all issue a fixed "legal share" of 25% (to be divided between issue) of what they would have received under intestacy (same as for a spouse/civil partner noted above); and

- Option 2 suggested that rather than a fixed entitlement to the estate, such dependents be provided with an amount that would provide for their ongoing maintenance, in circumstances where their other legal parent is not the person receiving the deceased's estate.

In practice, Option 2 would be where a person, A, dies leaving a dependent child, B, and A leaves their estate to various parties, none of whom are B or B's second legal parent.

Should the distinction between heritable & moveable be removed?

The proposals for the "legal share" for a spouse/civil partner and "option 1" for the issue were based on a percentage share of the whole estate – i.e. without any distinction between heritable and moveable estate.

Chapter 3B looked specifically at whether any exemptions should be made in respect of "agricultural units" and, if so, how such exemptions would operate and the specific definitions of the exempt "units".

In the questions they focussed on whether exemptions should be made where giving a legal share "compromise the commercial viability of the business"[282].

Response to the 2015 consultation

The key theme to the Government's Response[283] was that there was very little consensus on the various questions asked and that responses were generally divided.

The main section from the Response reads:

> "*The current scheme of legal rights attracts criticism but it does have the benefit of striking a balance between testamentary freedom and limited protections for spouses/civil partners and children. Further encroachment on the autonomy of individuals would undermine their ability to manage their affairs as they wish. The alternative consulted on would attract a greater degree of criticism than the current system given the lack of consensus about children's rights and because of the viability concerns about the impact of the removal of the distinction between heritable and moveable estate on certain land based businesses. On that basis we do not intend to bring forward reforms in this area.*"[284]

As such, although various proposals and suggestions were put forward to potentially reform legal rights in Scotland, the Government opted not to undertake reform in respect of who can claim, how much they would be entitled to or whether to include heritable property.

---

282 Ib id, at page 40.

283 See: Scottish Law Commission: *Scottish Government response to the Consultation on the Law of Succession.*

284 Ib id at page 9.

When the Consultation in 2019 opened, it focussed on the law of intestacy (and other parties' rights) and confirmed the position that there would be no such reform on legal rights.

An ongoing debate?

Despite the Government opting not to undertake reform there does remain an ongoing debate in the legal profession as to whether legal rights, in their current form, ought to continue.

There are those who have very strong opinions on the matter and believe a person should have full testamentary freedom to determine how their estate is to be divided, and that it is wrong to have this system of forced heirship. Many feel that where there is an adult child who has been estranged from the deceased and has their own wealth, is not in need of protection and the blanket rule for legal rights shouldn't apply in these scenarios.

Others feel very strongly that there should be legal protections in place to ensure certain parties are not unjustly disinherited. Some of the scenarios practitioners have seen will include where there is a second marriage and the whole estate is left to the new spouse/civil partner, who has no obligation to leave anything to the deceased's original children, or where there is a minor child whose parent hadn't adequately provided for them in life, or, scenarios where a spouse/civil partner/child has been the victim of domestic abuse and left the family home for their own protection.

There are valid arguments on both sides of the debate and it appears this may continue long into the future.

The system south of the border

In contrast to legal rights, the system in England and Wales does not give any party a fixed entitlement to an estate.

Instead, under the Inheritance (Provision for Family and Dependants) Act 1975, certain parties may make a claim to an estate and the value will be determined by a Court.

The parties entitled are broader than those who would be entitled to legal rights, and as the amount due is dependent on the facts and circumstances of each case, there is no certainty as to what a Court may deem appropriate.

Some practitioners have argued that this system is fairer as it means a court would judge whether a party ought to be entitled to inherit or not, and there would not be a "one size fits all" approach, as there is with legal rights.

That said, it also means that testators have less control in terms of planning their estate as any such claims are outwith their control, whereas with legal rights testators know how these are calculated and can take advice and steps to avoid or reduce potential claims.

Will we see changes?

As modern families no longer represent the historic "nuclear family" that existed when legal rights originated, it is possible that there will be public pressure for reform at some point in the future.

That said, because opinions are so divided between practitioners, and the Scottish public in the present, it seems legal rights will continue for the time being, and there's certainly nothing on the Scottish Government's agenda to push for reform in this area.

Practitioners should therefore continue to be mindful of the impact of legal rights when advising on succession planning, and when advising executors or potential claimants on a death.

MORE BOOKS BY LAW BRIEF PUBLISHING

A selection of our other titles available now:-

'A Practical Guide to Transgender Law' by Robin Moira White & Nicola Newbegin
'Artificial Intelligence – The Practical Legal Issues (2nd Edition)' by John Buyers
'A Practical Guide to Challenging Sham Marriage Allegations in Immigration Law' by Priya Solanki
'A Practical Guide to New Build Conveyancing' by Paul Sams & Rebecca East
'A Practical Guide to Inherited Wealth on Divorce' by Hayley Trim
'A Practical Guide to Shareholder Disputes in Family Businesses' by Ed Weeks
'A Practical Guide to the Law of Forests in Scotland' by Philip Buchan
'A Practical Guide to Health and Medical Cases in Immigration Law' by Rebecca Chapman & Miranda Butler
'A Practical Guide to Bad Character Evidence for Criminal Practitioners by Aparna Rao
'A Practical Guide to Environmental Enforcement' by Christopher Badger & Stuart Jessop
'A Practical Guide to Hoarding and Mental Health for Housing Lawyers' by Rachel Coyle
'A Practical Guide to Psychiatric Claims in Personal Injury – 2nd Edition' by Liam Ryan
'Stephens on Contractual Indemnities' by Richard Stephens
'A Practical Guide to the EU Succession Regulation' by Richard Frimston
'A Practical Guide to Solicitor and Client Costs – 2nd Edition' by Robin Dunne
'Constructive Dismissal – Practice Pointers and Principles' by Benjimin Burgher
'A Practical Guide to Religion and Belief Discrimination Claims in the Workplace' by Kashif Ali
'A Practical Guide to the Law of Medical Treatment Decisions' by Ben Troke

'Fundamental Dishonesty and QOCS in Personal Injury Proceedings: Law and Practice' by Jake Rowley

'A Practical Guide to the Law in Relation to School Exclusions' by Charlotte Hadfield & Alice de Coverley

'A Practical Guide to Divorce for the Silver Separators' by Karin Walker

'The Right to be Forgotten – The Law and Practical Issues' by Melissa Stock

'A Practical Guide to Planning Law and Rights of Way in National Parks, the Broads and AONBs' by James Maurici QC, James Neill et al

'A Practical Guide to Election Law' by Tom Tabori

'A Practical Guide to the Law in Relation to Surrogacy' by Andrew Powell

'A Practical Guide to Claims Arising from Fatal Accidents – 2nd Edition' by James Patience

'A Practical Guide to the Ownership of Employee Inventions – From Entitlement to Compensation' by James Tumbridge & Ashley Roughton

'A Practical Guide to Asbestos Claims' by Jonathan Owen & Gareth McAloon

'A Practical Guide to Stamp Duty Land Tax in England and Northern Ireland' by Suzanne O'Hara

'A Practical Guide to the Law of Farming Partnerships' by Philip Whitcomb

'Covid-19, Homeworking and the Law – The Essential Guide to Employment and GDPR Issues' by Forbes Solicitors

'Covid-19, Force Majeure and Frustration of Contracts – The Essential Guide' by Keith Markham

'Covid-19 and Criminal Law – The Essential Guide' by Ramya Nagesh

'Covid-19 and Family Law in England and Wales – The Essential Guide' by Safda Mahmood

'A Practical Guide to the Law of Unlawful Eviction and Harassment – 2nd Edition' by Stephanie Lovegrove

'Covid-19, Residential Property, Equity Release and Enfranchisement – The Essential Guide' by Paul Sams and Louise Uphill

'Covid-19, Brexit and the Law of Commercial Leases – The Essential Guide' by Mark Shelton

'A Practical Guide to Costs in Personal Injury Claims – 2nd Edition' by Matthew Hoe

'A Practical Guide to the General Data Protection Regulation (GDPR) – 2nd Edition' by Keith Markham
'Ellis on Credit Hire – Sixth Edition' by Aidan Ellis & Tim Kevan
'A Practical Guide to Working with Litigants in Person and McKenzie Friends in Family Cases' by Stuart Barlow
'Protecting Unregistered Brands: A Practical Guide to the Law of Passing Off' by Lorna Brazell
'A Practical Guide to Secondary Liability and Joint Enterprise Post-Jogee' by Joanne Cecil & James Mehigan
'A Practical Guide to the Pre-Action RTA Claims Protocol for Personal Injury Lawyers' by Antonia Ford
'A Practical Guide to Neighbour Disputes and the Law' by Alexander Walsh
'A Practical Guide to Forfeiture of Leases' by Mark Shelton
'A Practical Guide to Coercive Control for Legal Practitioners and Victims' by Rachel Horman
'A Practical Guide to Rights Over Airspace and Subsoil' by Daniel Gatty
'Tackling Disclosure in the Criminal Courts – A Practitioner's Guide' by Narita Bahra QC & Don Ramble
'A Practical Guide to the Law of Driverless Cars – Second Edition' by Alex Glassbrook, Emma Northey & Scarlett Milligan
'A Practical Guide to TOLATA Claims' by Greg Williams
'A Practical Guide to Elderly Law – 2nd Edition' by Justin Patten
'A Practical Guide to the Law of Prescription in Scotland' by Andrew Foyle
'A Practical Guide to the Construction and Rectification of Wills and Trust Instruments' by Edward Hewitt
'A Practical Guide to the Law of Bullying and Harassment in the Workplace' by Philip Hyland
'How to Be a Freelance Solicitor: A Practical Guide to the SRA-Regulated Freelance Solicitor Model' by Paul Bennett
'A Practical Guide to Prison Injury Claims' by Malcolm Johnson
'A Practical Guide to the Small Claims Track - 2nd Edition' by Dominic Bright
'A Practical Guide to Advising Clients at the Police Station' by Colin Stephen McKeown-Beaumont

'A Practical Guide to Antisocial Behaviour Injunctions' by Iain Wightwick
'Practical Mediation: A Guide for Mediators, Advocates, Advisers, Lawyers, and Students in Civil, Commercial, Business, Property, Workplace, and Employment Cases' by Jonathan Dingle with John Sephton
'The Mini-Pupillage Workbook' by David Boyle
'A Practical Guide to Crofting Law' by Brian Inkster
'A Practical Guide to Spousal Maintenance' by Liz Cowell
'A Practical Guide to the Law of Domain Names and Cybersquatting' by Andrew Clemson
'A Practical Guide to the Law of Gender Pay Gap Reporting' by Harini Iyengar
'A Practical Guide to the Rights of Grandparents in Children Proceedings' by Stuart Barlow
'NHS Whistleblowing and the Law' by Joseph England
'Employment Law and the Gig Economy' by Nigel Mackay & Annie Powell
'A Practical Guide to Noise Induced Hearing Loss (NIHL) Claims' by Andrew Mckie, Ian Skeate, Gareth McAloon
'An Introduction to Beauty Negligence Claims – A Practical Guide for the Personal Injury Practitioner' by Greg Almond
'Intercompany Agreements for Transfer Pricing Compliance' by Paul Sutton
'Zen and the Art of Mediation' by Martin Plowman
'A Practical Guide to the SRA Principles, Individual and Law Firm Codes of Conduct 2019 – What Every Law Firm Needs to Know' by Paul Bennett
'A Practical Guide to Adoption for Family Lawyers' by Graham Pegg
'A Practical Guide to Industrial Disease Claims' by Andrew Mckie & Ian Skeate
'A Practical Guide to Redundancy' by Philip Hyland
'A Practical Guide to Vicarious Liability' by Mariel Irvine
'A Practical Guide to Applications for Landlord's Consent and Variation of Leases' by Mark Shelton
'A Practical Guide to Relief from Sanctions Post-Mitchell and Denton' by Peter Causton
'A Practical Guide to Equity Release for Advisors' by Paul Sams
'A Practical Guide to Financial Services Claims' by Chris Hegarty

'The Law of Houses in Multiple Occupation: A Practical Guide to HMO Proceedings' by Julian Hunt
'Occupiers, Highways and Defective Premises Claims: A Practical Guide Post-Jackson – 2nd Edition' by Andrew Mckie
'A Practical Guide to Financial Ombudsman Service Claims' by Adam Temple & Robert Scrivenor
'A Practical Guide to Advising Schools on Employment Law' by Jonathan Holden
'A Practical Guide to Running Housing Disrepair and Cavity Wall Claims: 2nd Edition' by Andrew Mckie & Ian Skeate
'A Practical Guide to Holiday Sickness Claims – 2nd Edition' by Andrew Mckie & Ian Skeate
'Arguments and Tactics for Personal Injury and Clinical Negligence Claims' by Dorian Williams
'A Practical Guide to Drone Law' by Rufus Ballaster, Andrew Firman, Eleanor Clot
'A Practical Guide to Compliance for Personal Injury Firms Working With Claims Management Companies' by Paul Bennett
'RTA Allegations of Fraud in a Post-Jackson Era: The Handbook – 2nd Edition' by Andrew Mckie
'RTA Personal Injury Claims: A Practical Guide Post-Jackson' by Andrew Mckie
'On Experts: CPR35 for Lawyers and Experts' by David Boyle
'An Introduction to Personal Injury Law' by David Boyle
'A Practical Guide to Subtle Brain Injury Claims' by Pankaj Madan

These books and more are available to order online direct from the publisher at www.lawbriefpublishing.com, where you can also read free sample chapters. For any queries, contact us on 0844 587 2383 or mail@lawbriefpublishing.com.

Our books are also usually in stock at www.amazon.co.uk with free next day delivery for Prime members, and at good legal bookshops such as Wildy & Sons.

We are regularly launching new books in our series of practical day-to-day practitioners' guides. Visit our website and join our free newsletter to be kept informed and to receive special offers, free chapters, etc.

You can also follow us on Twitter at www.twitter.com/lawbriefpub.

www.ingramcontent.com/pod-product-compliance
Lightning Source LLC
LaVergne TN
LVHW022036200926
848481LV00003B/705
* 9 7 8 1 9 1 4 6 0 8 1 3 1 *